101
BATHROOM
BOREDOM
BUSTING
Activities

Brainteasers by G. L. Moore
Crafts by Courtney Sanchez
Fun Facts & Jokes by Heidi Fiedler
Illustrated by Santiago Gutierrez

Brimming with creative inspiration, how-to projects, and useful information to enrich your everyday life, Quarto Knows is a favorite destination for those pursuing their interests and passions. Visit our site and dig deeper with our books into your area of interest: Quarto Creates, Quarto Cooks, Quarto Homes, Quarto Lives, Quarto Drives, Quarto Explores, Quarto Gifts, or Quarto Kids.

© 2016 Quarto Publishing Group USA Inc.

First Published in 2016 by Walter Foster Jr., an imprint of The Quarto Group.
6 Orchard Road, Suite 100, Lake Forest, CA 92630, USA.
T (949) 380-7510 **F** (949) 380-7575 **www.QuartoKnows.com**

Walter Foster Jr. titles are also available at discount for retail, wholesale, promotional, and bulk purchase. For details, contact the Special Sales Manager by email at specialsales@quarto.com or by mail at The Quarto Group, Attn: Special Sales Manager, 401 Second Avenue North, Suite 310, Minneapolis, MN 55401 USA.

ISBN: 978-1-63322-081-2

Cover design by Santiago Gutierrez
Brainteasers written by G. L. Moore
Crafts by Courtney Sanchez
Illustrated by Santiago Gutierrez
Edited by Heidi Fiedler

Printed in China
10 9 8 7 6 5 4 3

101
BATHROOM
BOREDOM
BUSTING
Activities

CONTENTS

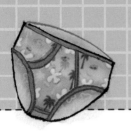

ANSWER KEY (PAGES 121–128)

CRAFTS (PAGES 129–176)

DO YOU POO?
HERE'S WHAT TO DO.

Babies. Boys. Girls.
Gorillas. Presidents.
Even princesses. We all poo!

Sometimes a lot. Sometimes a little. But poo, we do!
By now, you're probably a pooing pro. You know where
the toilet paper is and how to flush a big turd way,
way down. After reading every word on the shampoo
bottle and counting all the polka dots on the bathmat,
you've got this. In fact, maybe the only secret no one
has told you about pooing is that it can be boring. Next
time it's your turn to visit the bathroom, try one of the
brainteasers, puzzles, or crafts in this book. There are 101
activities, so every time you hit the toilet, you can turn
an ordinary chore into a plip plop poo party.

Poo on, friends! Poo on!

PUZZLES AND BRAINTEASERS

Now there's more to think about in the bathroom than whether or not to scrunch or fold the toilet paper! The puzzles and brainteasers in this book are designed to keep your brain busy while your body does its thing. Each of the puzzles and brainteasers has been rated in difficulty on the Stink-O-Meter from easy to hard. You'll find these ratings at the top of each page. Whether you're taking a quick pee or a leisurely poo, there's an activity just right for you.

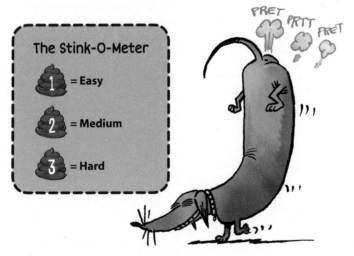

The Stink-O-Meter

1 = Easy

2 = Medium

3 = Hard

Challenge yourself to solve each of these puzzles, and you'll walk out of the bathroom feeling accomplished in more ways than one.

#1 BATHROOM DETECTIVE

When you're unloading in the bathroom, you don't want any distractions. It helps to have a place for everything and everything in its place. The toilet below needs some serious help before it will be ready to catch a glob of poo. Compare it to the other setups, and circle the difference in each picture.

THE ROYAL ROOM

Called everything from the *Commode* to the *Porcelain Throne*, there are over 100 names for the bathroom. Our favorite is the *Reading Room*.

Philosophers agree, "I poo therefore I am."

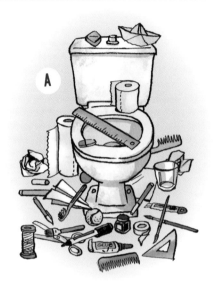

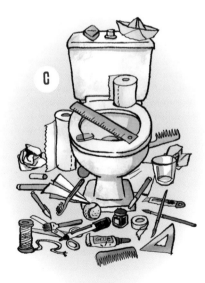

ANSWERS ON PAGE 121

#2 TOOT, TOOT!

1

There's no doubt that whoever smelt it, dealt it, but there's lots of debate about what to call "it." There are a gut-busting number of ways to say "someone has emitted a noise from their bottom." How many can you find in this pair of underpants? They run in straight lines in any direction, including diagonally, forward, and backward.

Puzzles and Brainteasers

```
R R E A R R A S P B E R R Y R
L B O W E L B L A S T H N I E
T U U R E F A R T P E O P I A
I R T T S T R U M P I P E F G
R U E E T F E P C S E C F A R
S H B F R B X X L R S U S W A
  P A F E U U H F H L I
  R R I P R C C E N
  A X H F P A D
  E P K W K P S
```

- [ ] Bowel blast
- [ ] Butt burp
- [ ] Chuff
- [ ] Expulsion
- [ ] Fart
- [ ] Gas leak
- [ ] Rear raspberry
- [ ] Ripper
- [ ] Whiffer
- [ ] Wind

PRRRTT

FART SPRAY

FUN FACT

On average, people let it rip 10 times every day!

Do you know your ones from your twos? Fill in these puzzles so every row and column contains the numbers 1, 2, 3, and 4.

All neighboring squares that have a difference of 2 have a log of poo between them. For example, when there's a 1 next to a 3, there is a log of poo between them, because the difference between 1 and 3 is 2. There are also poo logs between the neighboring 2s and 4s, but not between any other numbers.

1	4	2	3
4	3	1	2
2	1	3	4
3	2	4	1

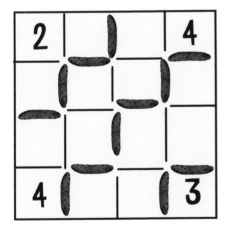

	3	4	
	2	3	

NUMBER THREES

Going number one is peeing. Number two is poo. But did you know there's also a number three? Liquid poo!

#4 TOILET PAPER CHAINS

Over or under? The debate about the correct way to load the toilet paper rages on. Some swear it's easier to grab a square from the top of the TP. Others believe the paper should hang from the bottom. Take time to think about which side you're on—and you MUST take a side—while you complete each toilet-paper chain. Convert the top word into the bottom word, one sheet at a time, changing only one letter at a time.

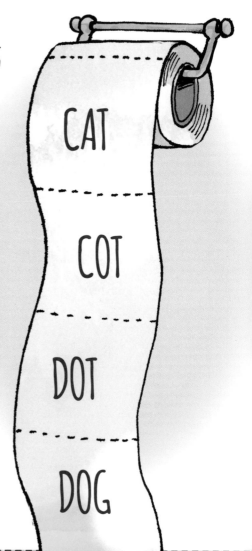

CAT

COT

DOT

DOG

SIGN LANGUAGE

If you find yourself in a Japanese bathroom, you might be confused by the enormous number of buttons on your toilet. Each one presents a way to customize your ride. Use this chart to brush up on your Japanese before the bidet sprays where the sun don't shine.

Stop 停止
Spray スプレー
Bidet ビデ
Water Pressure 水圧
Sound 聞こえる
Volume ボリューム
Deodorizer 脱臭剤

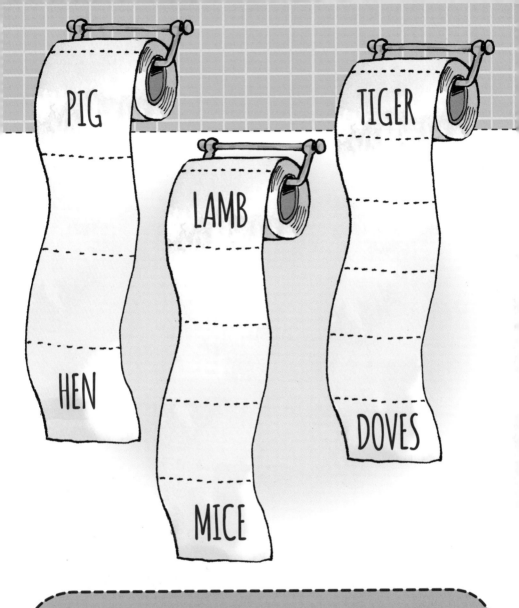

PIG

HEN

LAMB

MICE

TIGER

DOVES

THE RIGHT WIPE

Is it better to scrunch the toilet paper into a ball or fold it into a neat pile? Scrunchers say a loose ball of paper is faster and prevents hand-to-poo contact. Folders say the only way to get really clean is to use a flat surface. What's your wipe style?

ANSWERS ON PAGE 121

#5 GREAT POO MOUNTAIN

Have you ever looked down in the toilet to admire your work and seen a humongous mountain of poo staring back at you? Your first thought might be "How the heck did THAT come out of me?" But your second thought is surely one of pride. "I made that!" You ate a mound of food, digested it like a beast, and then produced your very own mountain of poo. Well done! Draw a path between the mountains on this page following these rules.

RULES

• You can only draw horizontal or vertical lines, and each mountain must use exactly the same number of lines as the number on the mountain.

• Lines can't cross each other or travel over a mountain.

• There can be no more than two lines directly joining any pair of mountains.

• You must arrange the set of lines so that someone could walk from one mountain to any other mountain, just using the lines you've drawn.

Example

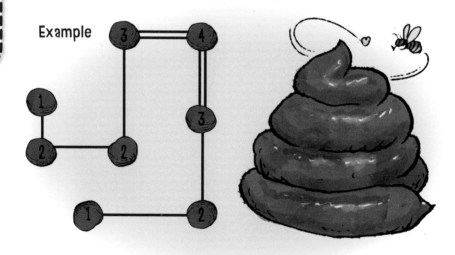

FUN FACT

Poo is made of water, mucus, dead cells, bacteria, fiber, fat, protein, and other food your body couldn't digest.

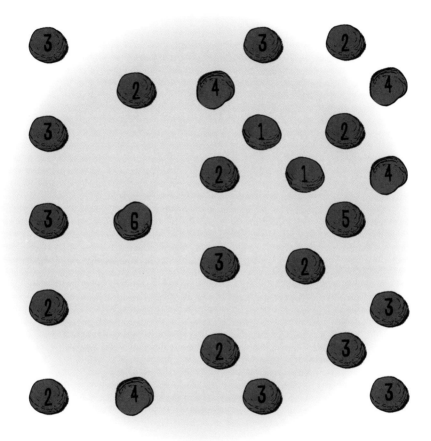

ALL TOGETHER NOW

Every day between 8 a.m. and 9 a.m., "the big flush sends wastewater racing through New York City's sewers. It's the most common time to go to the bathroom—at least in the city that never sleeps.

#6 OUT OF ORDER

Taking a massive poo can leave you feeling a lot lighter, and it's not just the relief that comes when the pressure to poo passes. It's possible to lose a pound after a long day of pooing. Looking at the pictures on the right, can you work out which shape is the heaviest, and which shape is the lightest?

Puzzles and Brainteasers

POUND FOR POUND

To see how much your poo weighs, you don't have to poo on the scale! Instead, weigh yourself before you poo and after. Then, compare the difference. That's how much your poo weighs.

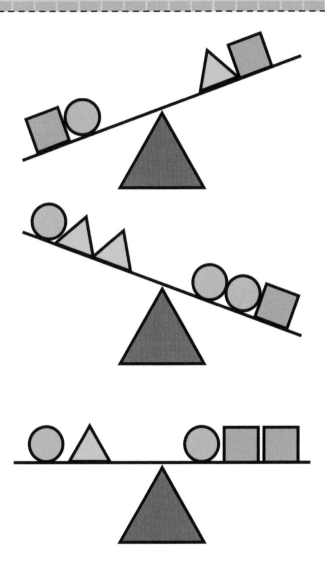

ANSWER ON PAGE 121

2

#7 POO PENNIES

We've all been there. You've released the perfect poo, and it's ready to travel through the pipes, out into the world. But when you reach for the TP—DISASTER strikes! Someone forgot to load a new roll. You search desperately, high and low, side to side. But there's nothing. Not a single square! Tissue? No! Cotton balls? No! You eye the clean towels and call for help. You're ready to negotiate. Allowance. Chores. You'll do whatever it takes to get someone—anyone—to pass you a roll of toilet paper. You know it's going to cost you, and you're prepared to pay. Answer the questions below to free yourself from the bathroom. Keep in mind that in The Land of Poo, there are coins of six different values:

1   2   5   10   20   50

1. What is the minimum number of coins you would need to buy a roll of TP that costs 9 cents?

2. What is the minimum number of coins you would need to buy a six-pack of TP for 73 cents?

3. You buy a plunger that costs 73 cents using two 50 cent coins. What is the smallest number of coins you can receive back if you are given exact change?

4. What is the maximum number of coins you can use to make up a total value of 35 cents if you use no more than two of any individual value of coin?

ANSWERS ON PAGE 121

#8 TARGET PRACTICE

Competitive pooers aim for the center of the bowl. Pick one number from each of the three rings on the target to make the totals below. For example, you could make a total of 36 by picking 6 from the innermost ring, 15 from the center ring, and 15 from the outermost ring. Fire away!

TARGET TOTALS

14

21

23

28

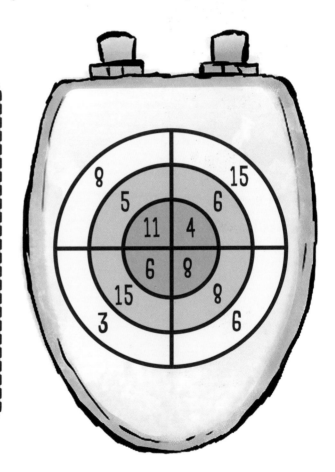

#9 CAUGHT SHORT

It's time to think fast! You're away from home, and you suddenly need the toilet. Can you find your way back home through this maze? Enter at the top and exit at the bottom. Some paths cross over and under each other, using the marked bridges. Hurry! The pressure's building!

FUN FACT

Food in the stomach triggers the intestines to get moving. That's why we often have to poo right after we eat. Yum!

A MAZE OF INTESTINES

After it has been chewed and swallowed, food moves from the mouth to the stomach. It winds through nearly 30 feet of intestines to reach the rectum. As waste travels through the body, the colon squeezes it dry and pulls out all the nutrients. When it gets to the end, food is finally poo.

TO TALK OR NOT TO TALK?

Everyone has an opinion. Is talking in the bathroom something that should never ever happen, or is it ok if it's someone you know? What if it's through the door? What if you need TP? Where do you stand (or sit) on this topic?

START

FINISH

ANSWER ON PAGE 122

#10 DIRTY LAUNDRY

At the end of the day, do you throw your dirty clothes on the bathroom floor or carefully place your clothes in the hamper? It might depend on what kind of day it was! By the looks of this floor, it was a very long day for this poor soul. At first glance, this underwear all looks the same, but there are actually small differences. There are two of each design. Draw lines to connect the pairs that match.

A

B

C

D

ANSWERS ON PAGE 122

E

F

G

H

EAU DE POO That rank smell radiating from your toilet is the smell of bacteria at work. Bacteria in our guts produce sulfur, which makes poo and gas smell like rotten eggs—or worse!

 # #11 THE TOOTHBRUSH TEST

A violent flush can spray itty bitty traces of poo around the room, so dentists recommend keeping your toothbrush more than six feet away from the toilet. You never really want to use someone else's toothbrush. But if you're at a sleepover and don't know how close your friends keep their toothbrushes to the toilet, you REALLY don't want to use someone else's toothbrush. Can you work out which brush is whose based on the statements to the right?

- Beatrice's is to the right of David's.
- David's is on an end.
- Abigail's is to the left of Charlotte's.
- Abigail's is not next to David's.

Toothbrush 1: _____

Toothbrush 2: _____

Toothbrush 3: _____

Toothbrush 4: _____

CORN, IS THAT YOU?

Most foods get chewed and digested into a brown mush. But some foods make it out looking alarmingly like the way they did going in. Corn, seeds, and celery can all make appearances that are difficult to forget if you see them staring back at you from your poo.

FUN FACT

Scientists use ancient poo to learn what dinosaurs, mammoths, and other animals ate millions of years ago.

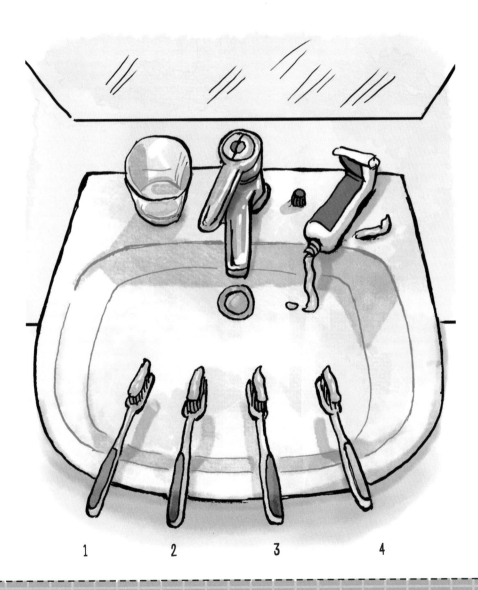

1   2   3   4

ANSWERS ON PAGE 122

#12 PASSING GAS

Are you a toilet poet and you just don't know it? The first step to crafting your own Ode to the Funky Farts is coming up with some creative ways to describe passing gas. List 10 ways to describe a fart. Extra points for grossness!

1 _____
2 _____
3 _____
4 _____
5 _____
6 _____
7 _____
8 _____
9 _____
10 _____

ODE TO THE FUNKY FARTS

Piff! Pop! Pow!
A round of gas can make you bow.
Eggs, cheese, beans.
All make your toots smell green and mean.
Down your throat.
Smell the effects of all that bloat.
Wait!
Why do my farts smell like art,
When the toots you toot make my nose fall apart?

#13 ON THE MOVE

Q: Why did the toilet paper
roll downhill?
A: To get to the bottom!

#14 THE POO POLICE

Some crooks broke into the police station and stole all their toilets. The police are investigating, but for now they have nothing to go on!

TP + Poo = the answer to a lot of life's problems, but too much of a good thing can cause a new problem. A massive poo or a wad of toilet paper can back up the pipes. In this sewer system, some of the pipes have gone missing. Can you find which pipe is needed to fill the holes and fix the system? You might need to rotate them to fit.

FUN FACT

With all those shiny, hard surfaces, bathrooms aren't just the perfect place to poo—they're also a great place to sing.

SIT OR SQUAT?

Unless you're a baby who just lies there as the poo rolls out, there are two main ways to take a poo. Some people sit on the toilet and others squat, either outside or on a special toilet. Doctors say squatting is the healthiest way to poo, but what you do is up to you!

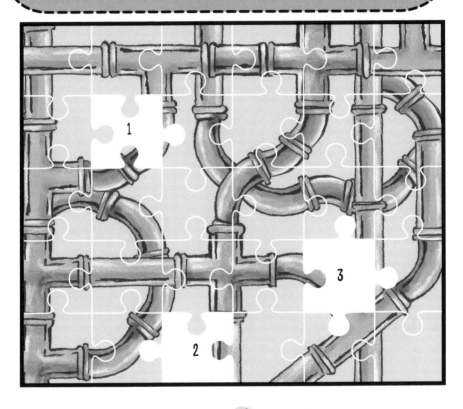

A

B

C

ANSWERS ON PAGE 122

#16 A FIVE-FLUSH TOILET

Quiet or loud? White walls or colorful art? A nightlight or a bright light? Everyone has their favorites. Use this chart to rate your bathroom experience.

Home:

_____ Interior Design _____ Smell _____ Soap _____ Cleanliness

_____ Privacy _____ Comfort _____ Toilet Paper _____ Total

Notes:_____

School:

_____ Interior Design _____ Smell _____ Soap _____ Cleanliness

_____ Privacy _____ Comfort _____ Toilet Paper _____ Total

Notes:_____

FUN FACT

Nearly 20 percent of Americans admit to peeing in the pool!

Friend's House:

_____ Interior Design _____ Smell _____ Soap _____ Cleanliness
_____ Privacy _____ Comfort _____ Toilet Paper _____ Total
Notes: _____

Park:

_____ Interior Design _____ Smell _____ Soap _____ Cleanliness
_____ Privacy _____ Comfort _____ Toilet Paper _____ Total
Notes: _____

Bookstore:

_____ Interior Design _____ Smell _____ Soap _____ Cleanliness
_____ Privacy _____ Comfort _____ Toilet Paper _____ Total
Notes: _____

Favorite Restaurant:

_____ Interior Design _____ Smell _____ Soap _____ Cleanliness
_____ Privacy _____ Comfort _____ Toilet Paper _____ Total
Notes: _____

Beach:

_____ Interior Design _____ Smell _____ Soap _____ Cleanliness
_____ Privacy _____ Comfort _____ Toilet Paper _____ Total
Notes: _____

Camp:

_____ Interior Design _____ Smell _____ Soap _____ Cleanliness
_____ Privacy _____ Comfort _____ Toilet Paper _____ Total
Notes: _____

Ancient Romans used public toilets with long rows of holes in the ground and a public sponge—used as toilet paper—that each person shared. Not so clean or private, but a good way to get to know your neighbors. In each puzzle below, the aim is to draw a single loop that joins some of the squares together using only horizontal or vertical lines. The loop can't enter a square more than once, which means it can't touch or cross over itself. The numbered squares in the puzzle grid tell you how many of their neighboring squares are used by the loop, including diagonally neighboring squares.

Example

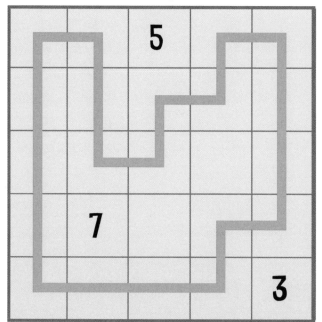

FUN FACT On average, people use 57 squares of toilet paper per day.

PUZZLE 1

	7			
			7	
3				

PUZZLE 2

4			5	
3				
				3

ANSWERS ON PAGE 122

#18 BATTLESHIP

Puzzles and Brainteasers

What makes a piece of poo float to the top or sink to the bottom of the toilet? Gas! Big gas bubbles can make poo so light, it can be hard to flush those stinkers down. That's when it's time to bring in the big guns. Battleship is usually played with two people, but this version is for just you. Can you find the five ships that have been hidden in the grid? Ships can only be placed horizontally or vertically, and they can't touch another ship (not even diagonally). The numbers on the edge of the grid tell you how many spaces in each row and column should contain ships.

Example

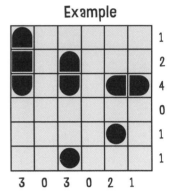

Hint: Some ship parts are already given to help you get going. Start by marking the squares you know must be empty, just like you would do for a "miss" in two-player Battleship.

Puzzle

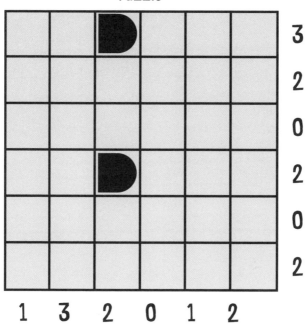

3
2
0
2
0
2

1 3 2 0 1 2

WHOOSH!

On a spaceship, even simple things like pooing become complicated. Astronauts use vacuums to collect their waste.

Battleships

ANSWER ON PAGE 122

It's always good to have a Plan B, and when you're in the bathroom, that means having a box or two of tissue on hand for emergencies. How many boxes can you count in each of these drawings? Don't forget to count the hidden ones at the back that must be holding up the boxes above them.

Example—5 Boxes

STANDING BY

If you can stick a roll of toilet paper on it, someone probably has. Everything from a wooden giraffe to a butler's arms has been used to store TP.

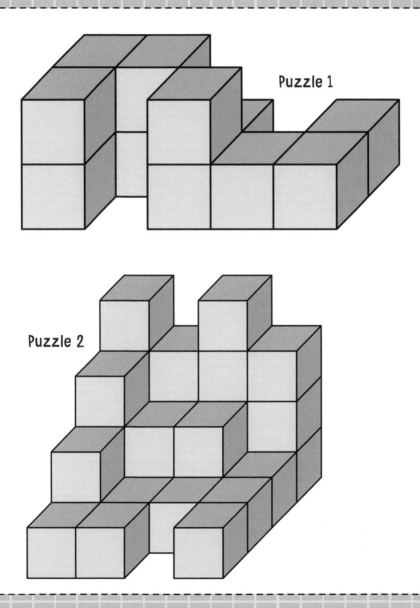

Puzzle 1

Puzzle 2

#20 COUNTING TILES

When sitting on the pot has gotten a little boring, you might find yourself counting the tiles on the floor (extra points for finding hidden patterns). In this activity, you'll draw along the dashed lines to divide each box into a set of rectangular bathrooms. Each bathroom must contain exactly one number, and that number must be equal to the number of floor tiles in the room.

Example

PUBLIC POETS

Today's public toilets are famous for their colorful graffiti, but the practice isn't new. Latin phrases like "Apollinaris, medicus Titi Imperatoris, hic cacavit bene" or "Apollinaris, doctor to the emperor Titus, had a good crap here" have been found on walls that are thousands of years old.

Puzzle 1

Puzzle 2

WIZ KID

If you're doing more than taking a wiz, you might be on the toilet a while, which makes it the perfect time to make some progress on this Sudoku puzzle. Place a number from 1 to 8 in each empty square. Arrange the numbers so that no number repeats in any row, column, or bold box. When you're done, pull up those smarty pants and give a celebratory flush!

Puzzles and Brainteasers

			6	2			
	2	5			1	8	
	3	2			7	4	
8							2
5							7
	1	3			6	2	
	6	8			4	1	
			1	3			

ANSWER ON PAGE 122

#22 POTTY MOUTH

1

Can you think of something found in the bathroom for each letter of the alphabet? For example, *A* could be *air freshener* and *B* could be *bubbles*. Try filling in the list to the right.

A _____
B _____
C _____
D _____
E _____
F _____
G _____
H _____
I _____
J _____
K _____
L _____
M _____
N _____
O _____
P _____
Q _____
R _____
S _____
T _____
U _____
V _____
W _____
X _____
Y _____
Z _____

#23 MEMORY MATCH

A full bathtub clocks in at around 35 gallons of water. A shower can use up to 5 gallons a minute. The average person flushes nearly 10,000 gallons of water per year. When it comes to bathrooms, numbers matter. Look at this list of numbers for 30 seconds, then cover it with a piece of toilet paper. Now write as many numbers as you can remember on a separate piece of paper. Once you've done that, uncover the list and see how many you remembered correctly.

9	91	7
19	13	73
3	35	55

FUN FACT
Snakes, squirrels, and small possums have all been known to show up swimming in toilets!

Puzzles and Brainteasers

PEE, POO, AND NOT MUCH ELSE

Carrots. Wipes. Goldfish. They've all been found in sewer treatment plants—whole. The packaging may say they're flushable, but sewers say differently when they send brown sludge back up the pipes. Plumbers say "If it doesn't come apart in your hands, don't flush it."

POO PIE

Dogs and other animals sometimes eat their own poo. It's a good way to get any nutrients they might have missed the first time around.

PRO TIP

Boys
Stand closer for better aim!

Girls
Stay seated the whole time!

 # #24 DOODIE DOODLES

Staring at a used tissue can be like looking at an abstract painting. You might see a butterfly or a storm cloud, depending how you look at it. Each doodle below has been drawn twice. Can you match each doodle up with its mirror image?

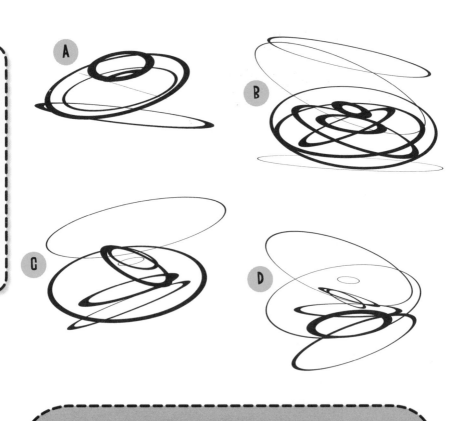

AUTO FLUSH NIGHTMARES

Despite the loud whoosh and bad timing that may accompany it, auto flush is never feared by real bathroom pros, for it is there to keep our hands clean and our toilets cleaner. So repeat after me "Auto flush is our friend. Auto flush is our friend."

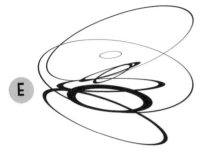

E

F

G

H

ANSWERS ON PAGE 122

3

Imagine you have to build your own portable outhouse. To make it modern you'll make it square, of course. The flat designs to the right can be folded to make six-sided cubes.

Puzzles and Brainteasers

But two patterns that will never make an outhouse are mixed up with the correct ones. Without actually cutting the designs out, can you work out which two are the odd ones out?

WC

#26 LOOSE VOWELS

Some people feel like they have to poo when they're in a bookstore. Maybe the smell of the books affects their poo muscles. Others think the urge comes when you're standing and relaxed, whether you're looking at books or something else. Or maybe it's just that lots of people read in the bathroom and seeing all those books reminds them they need to go! Either way, books and the letters in them are definitely connected to poo. In this activity, all the vowels have been washed out of the following words, which are all things you might find in a bathroom. Can you figure out what the original words were?

TTHBRSH

SHWR

TWL

TLT

CMB

FCT

ANSWERS ON PAGE 123

#27 DIRTY DOMINOES

Dominoes may not officially be the game of kings, but if it's good enough for King Tut, it's probably good enough for you and your porcelain throne. A full set of dominoes contains 28 different designs, with 1 to 6 or a blank on each end of every domino. By drawing along the dashed lines, can you reveal the full set of all 28 dominoes? This means that every possible domino will appear exactly once. Some are marked for you already, and there's a chart to keep track of which dominoes you've already found.

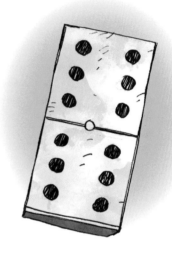

Example

1	5	3	1	4	4	3	4
6	2		1	5	5		4
3		6	6		1	5	4
2		5	6	6	6	3	1
2	4	3		5	1	4	3
3	3	2	6	4		5	1
2	6	2	2		2	1	5

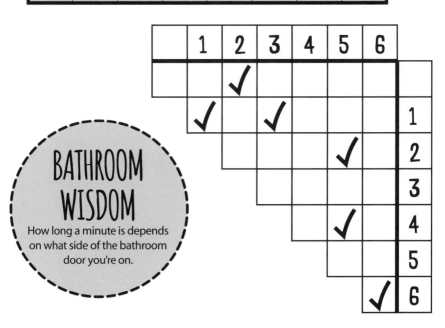

ANSWERS ON PAGE 123

Crisscross applesauce may not be the most obvious way to sit on the toilet, but sometimes when you're in the bathroom, you have to get creative. Can you solve these puzzles by crisscrossing your cotton swabs? To make things easier, use your pencil to draw lines representing each swab.

EXAMPLE
If you have four cotton swabs, you can arrange them to make one square by laying them out like this.

Puzzle 1

Imagine you have six cotton swabs. What is the maximum number of squares you can make all at once with these six cotton swabs? If you think the answer with six swabs is still one square, you're missing something! There's actually a way of making more than one square with just six swabs.

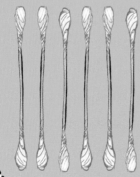

FUN FACT

At the 2005 London Marathon, runner Paula Radcliffe stopped on the side of the road to poop in front of the live crowd and TV cameras. She went on to win the race, but when you gotta go, you gotta go.

Puzzle 2

What's the maximum number of squares you can make with just eight cotton swabs? Here's a clue: it's more than 10!

 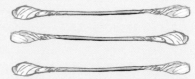

ANSWERS ON PAGE 123

#29 ARTSY TP

There's no real reason toilet paper needs to come on a round tube—unless you want it to roll easily. A hexagon or pentagon tube would work too. The TP just might not come off as smoothly. This picture shows a variety of unusually shaped empty rolls of TP from above. Each picture is shown twice, but in each case different parts of it are covered with white squares of paper. Combine both images to complete the picture. How many hexagons are there? How many pentagons?

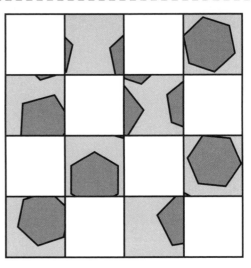

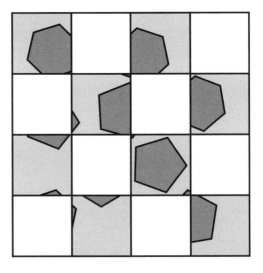

Pentagons: _____   Hexagons: _____

#31 REFLECTIONS

Chances are your bathroom routine includes a long glance in the mirror. But have you ever thought about what's actually happening when you look in the mirror? A mirror is really just a shiny piece of glass with a metal back that reflects images. Use your experience with mirrors to work out which of the images to your right reflects each image on top.

FUN FACT Collectors pay top dollar for fossilized dino poo. Some pieces clock in at 40 inches long and sell for nearly $10,000!

PURPOSEFUL POO

When many animals poo, they do more than just get rid of waste. For example, storks poo on their legs to cool off on hot days, and tigers mark their territory with piles of poo.

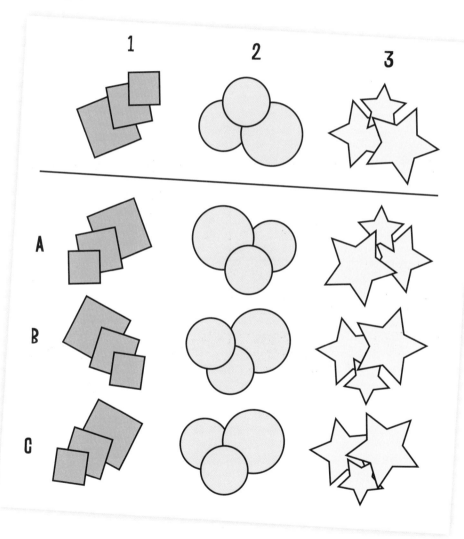

#32 BATHROOM BOTHER

Stinky. Crowded. No privacy. Those words may describe pretty much every public bathroom in the world. But every bathroom is also slightly different. There are 10 differences between these two very similar bathroom scenes. Can you find all 10?

DIGITAL POO

The poo emoji was first created in Japan, and people loved it. But American engineers weren't so sure about adding it to the US texting alphabet. At first people thought it was a swirl of chocolate ice cream. Or just too gross to use. But today the poo emoji is one of the most popular emojis in the world.

ANSWERS ON PAGE 123

#33 CHOCOLATE LOG-DOKU

Just like each piece of food you eat adds up to create the log of poo that comes out the other end, the letters *A* through *E* work together to form a Logidoku puzzle. Fill in each empty square so that you have one each of every letter from *A* to *E* in each row, column, and bold shape.

FUN FACT

Energy released from the gas in dog poo is being used to power a streetlamp in Massachusetts! Visit this first ever "Park Spark Project" where it stands at a dog park on Tudor St. in Cambridge.

ANSWER ON PAGE 123

#34 IN AND OUT

Help! Someone's let off a stinky one and you have to get away!

How quickly can you find your way through this maze? Hurry, before the smell gets worse!

START

FINISH

Puzzle 1

Did you know there's a relationship between peeing and pooing? We use muscles to control the flow of both, but the muscles that control our poo are stronger. That's why we often pee when we poo, but don't always poo when we pee. Can you work out the relationship between these numbers?

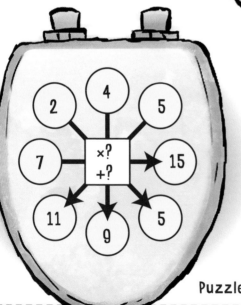

The number and symbol that replace each question mark transforms each number on the left into the number across from it. The second puzzle has a relationship with two steps. First you multiply by a number, then you add another number.

Puzzle 2

ANSWERS ON PAGE 124

THE BATHROOM BOOGIE

How do you make a tissue dance?

Put a little boogie in it!

BATHROOM JOKE!

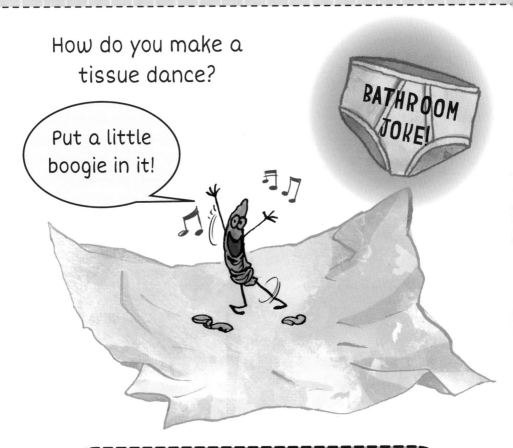

THAT'S WHAT FRIENDS ARE FOR

Doctors perform "fecal transplants" when someone is infected with *Clostridium difficile*. Unfortunately, it's exactly what it sounds like. A healthy person poos. The poo is stored. Doctors transfer the poo into someone who's not healthy. Then all the bacteria in that fresh poo helps fight off infection. It's a dirty job, but someone has to do it.

#37 ROMAN RELATIONS

The Romans were famous for their bathrooms, but they wrote number one and number two (along with all other numbers) differently. For example, I is 1, V is 5, X is 10, with other letters for higher numbers.

To solve this puzzle, place the numbers 1 to 6 once in every row, column, and bold rectangle of the grid. Wherever there is a V between two squares, then the numbers in those two squares must add up to 5. And wherever there is an X between two squares, the numbers in those two squares must add up to 10. Some numbers are given to get you going.

Puzzles and Brainteasers

#38 MEMORABLE FARTS

Look at this list of
words related to wind
for 30 seconds,
then cover it with
a piece of toilet paper.

Gust
Weather
Breeze
Gale
Hurricane
Windiness
Storm

PRRRRRT

Now look at the list on the left.
It contains the same words in a
different order. Using a separate
piece of toilet paper, can you
rewrite the words in the same
order as the first list?

Hurricane
Breeze
Storm
Gale
Gust
Windiness
Weather

BIGGER OR SMALLER

Puzzles and Brainteasers

There's no competition to produce the world's biggest poo—at least not yet. But that doesn't mean size doesn't matter in the bathroom. Complete this puzzle by placing a number from 1 to 4 in each empty square of toilet paper, so that each number appears once in every row and column. Some neighboring squares have ">" between them, which indicates that one of the numbers is greater than the other. The arrow always points to the smaller number.

Example

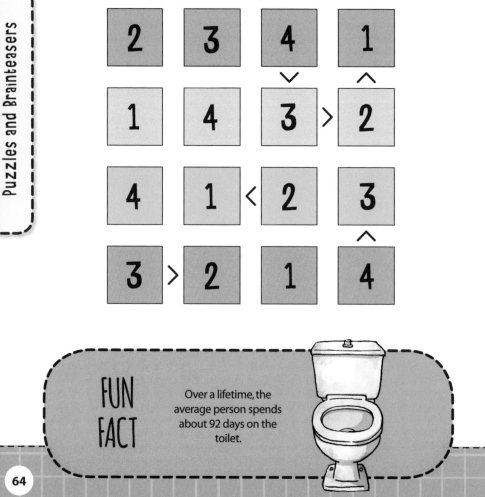

FUN FACT

Over a lifetime, the average person spends about 92 days on the toilet.

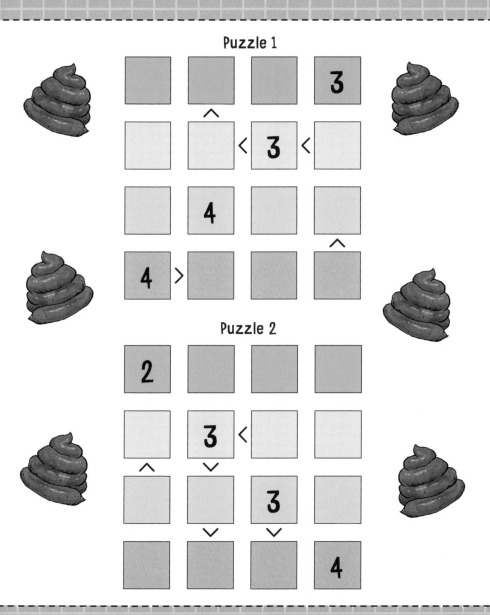

Puzzle 1

Puzzle 2

#40 TUSH TALK

If someone accuses you of farting, you might respond with, "He who accuses blew the fuses." But that might not be the end of it if your friend says, "Whoever said the rhyme, did the crime!" Now it's your turn. The rhymier your comeback, the funnier it will be.

If you need inspiration, try including one of these words in your reply.

Stinky • Whiffy • Hidden • Tooted • Farter • Loo

What did the toilet paper say when it landed in the water?

BATHROOM JOKE!

"That's how I roll!"

#42 WHAT AM I?

I've done my job,
When I wipe away a log.
I'm square,
But no one cares.
If I'm not there to help you dry,
You might just cry.
What am I?

ANSWER ON PAGE 124

#43 BATHROOM BINGO

1

Look around the bathroom and mark every item you can see from your spot on the pot. Complete a row across, up and down, or diagonally to win.

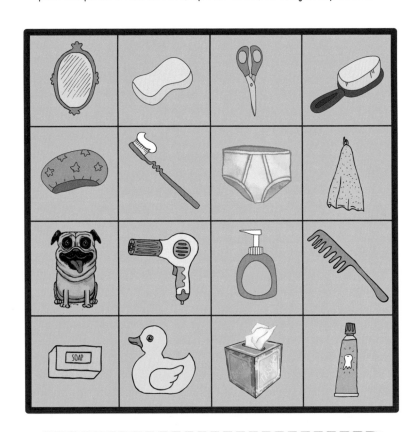

FUN FACT

The White House is home to 35 bathrooms!

#44 P.U.

How do you spell *smelly*? P.U.!
Write a letter from *A* to *F* in
each empty square, so that
no letter is repeated in any
row or column. Also, identical
letters can't touch one
another, not even diagonally.

FUN FACT
Fifteen percent of people
take their pants all the way
off to poo!

		D			
					F
				A	C
C	B				
F					
			F		

#45 EXIT PLAN

If you know you've got a poo emergency coming up, you'll want to know where all the bathrooms are no matter where you are. It can help to know how to read a floor plan, which is a map of a building. Using the walls that make up each of these floor plans, how many squares can you find? There will be various sizes, and some will include multiple rooms within them—including the large square all around the outside of the floor plan that contains *every* room! Once you've counted all the squares, now count all the rectangles too.

Puzzle 1

Squares: _____   Rectangles: _____

PRETTY PEES?

It may look pretty, but there's really only one color you want your pee to be: yellow. Here's what the other colors might mean. Your doctor can tell you more.

Clear You may be too hydrated
Pale yellow Healthy
Dark yellow You need to drink more water
Brown There may be old blood in your pee
Red or pink There may be fresh blood in your pee
Green You may be taking medicine

Puzzle 2

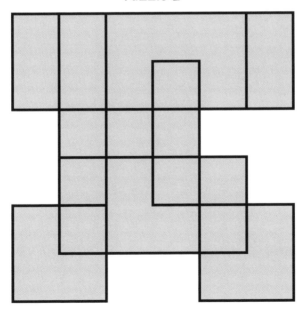

Squares: _____   Rectangles: _____

ANSWERS ON PAGE 124

There's really no good time or place to be clumsy, but being clumsy in the bathroom is the worst. You're sitting in position when…AH…AH…Choooooo! You sneeze, tumble off the pot, and send the TP flying. Now how are you going to get that roll of precious white paper from way over there to here? Very carefully, pulling the paper square by square closer to you. Breaking the chain would be a disaster. So how quickly can you solve each of these TP chains so they don't break? In each case, start with the number on the left and then apply each math operation in turn. What is the final result of each chain?

Puzzle 1

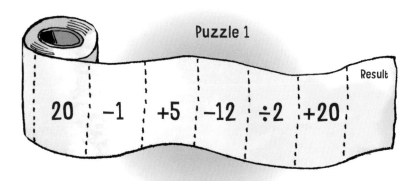

| 20 | −1 | +5 | −12 | ÷2 | +20 | Result |

Puzzle 2

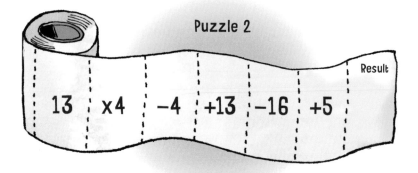

| 13 | x4 | −4 | +13 | −16 | +5 | Result |

Puzzle 3

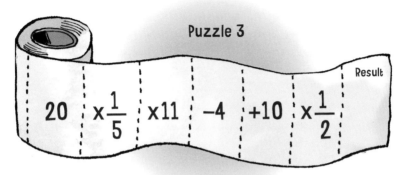

$20 \quad \times\dfrac{1}{5} \quad \times 11 \quad -4 \quad +10 \quad \times\dfrac{1}{2}$ — Result

BATHROOM BUDDIES

When you flush,
Don't blush.
Instead, take a bow,
Knowing I once sat
where you sit now.
For when we spend time in the loo,
There's nothing left to do but poo.
We may never meet,
But to share this sacred seat,
Well that's a friendship
that can't be beat!

POTTY TRAINING

When you're spraying air freshener, it's more about quantity than quality. But when it's time to pee, you want to aim more precisely. Use your time in the loo to keep your skills sharp. Draw lines on the grid to connect the matching shapes. The lines can't cross or touch each other, and only one line is allowed in each square. Diagonal lines aren't allowed.

Example

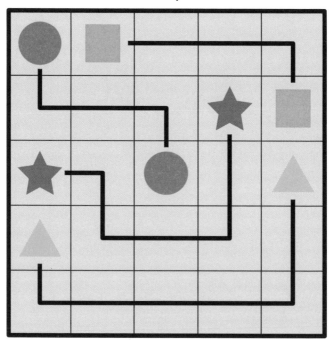

Puzzles and Brainteasers

FUN FACT
Thirty percent of people stand up to wipe.

FREE SPIRIT

Sing like no one is listening.
Love like you've never been hurt.
Dance like no one is watching.
Fart like no one can smell it.

Puzzle

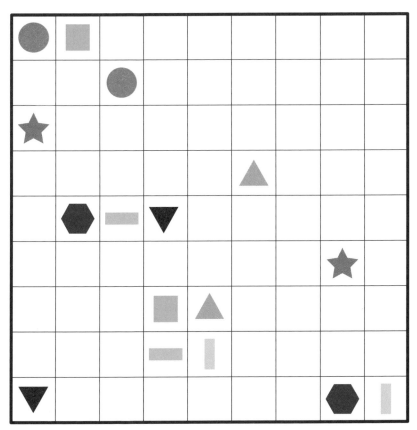

ANSWER ON PAGE 124

2

When it comes to poo, how well do you know your Starburst from your Bung Ball? Even experts can have trouble spotting the differences. Most of these boxes contain different sets of shapes. How many pairs of boxes containing identical symbols can you find?

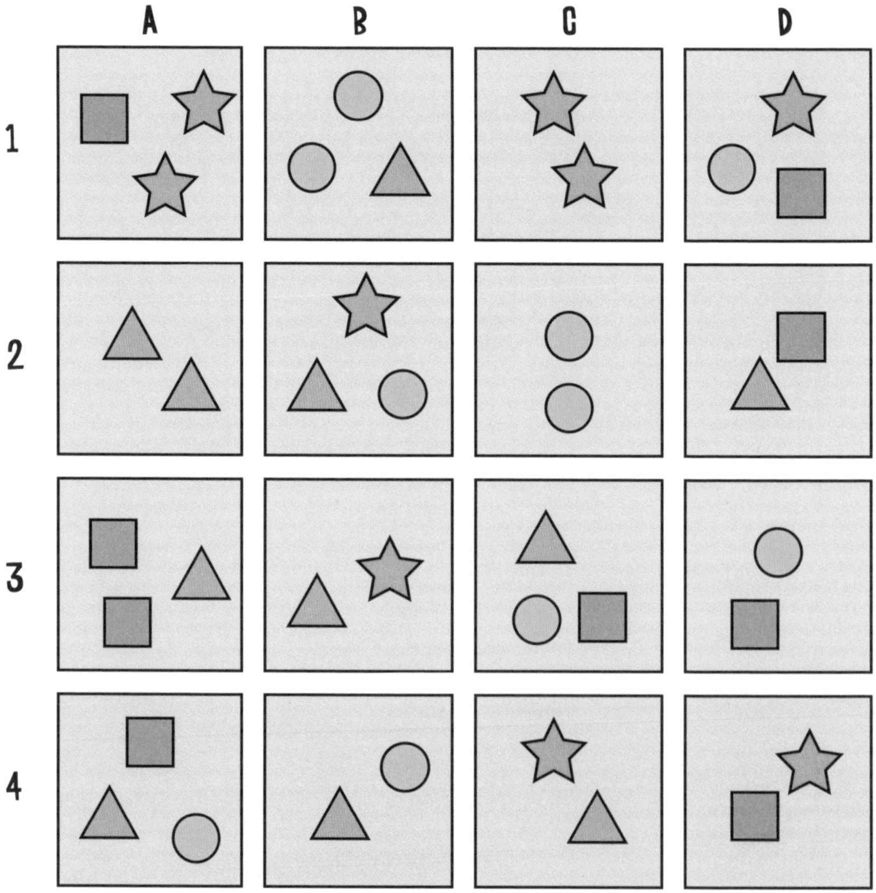

A   **B**   **C**   **D**

Puzzles and Brainteasers

1

2

3

4

THE POO RAINBOW

The color of your poo can reveal a lot about your health.
Doctors can tell you more!

Pink
could be a
sign you're eating
too many cherry
popsicles.

Red
means you ate
beets recently or
there could be some
blood in the poo.

Orange
means you may
have eaten carrots
or sweet potatoes
recently.

Yellow
may be a sign of
parasites.

Green
can be produced by
eating LOTS of green
vegetables.

Blue
is produced by
eating way too
much blue candy.

Brown
is as normal
as it gets.

Black
can be caused by
some medicines
or bleeding.

White
can be caused by some
medicines or a sign the liver
might not be working.

#49 ODD SHAPE OUT

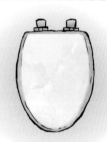

Most toilets are round, but others have been shaped to look like everything from trumpets to mouths! In this activity, find the toilet shape that doesn't belong with the others and explain why.

(Hint: You'll need to know more numbers than 1 and 2 to solve this one.)

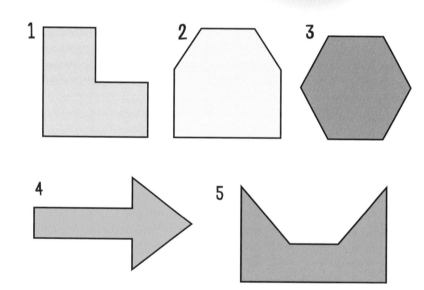

Puzzles and Brainteasers

CUSTOM COMMODE

Designers are working on a toilet that has multiple seats stacked on top of each other. When it's time to poo, each member of the family lifts the seats on top to reveal their own personal seat. Is this the future of toilets or just more to clean? You decide!

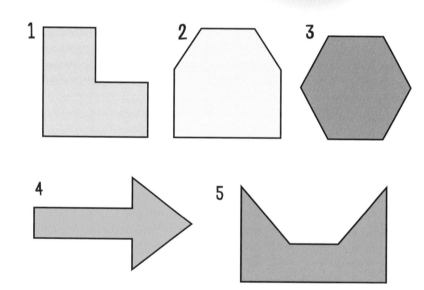

After doing 49 poo-tacular activities, you might start seeing poo everywhere—including your Sudoku board! Complete the grid by filling each empty square with either a number from 1 to 5 or a pile of poo. There must be one of each number and one poo in each row, column, and bold box.

	3				4
		💩			
4					
					3
			2		
1				💩	

FUN FACT The metal found in sewage each year could be worth up to 13 million dollars!

ANSWER ON PAGE 125

#51 POTTY PATTERNS

When you need to go to the bathroom, it's hard to think about anything else. "Potties! Potties! Potties! Find a potty!" your brain sounds the alarm as it scans for options. Keep your eyes sharp with this activity. The shapes form a pattern, but four shapes are missing. Which of the options to the right correctly completes the pattern?

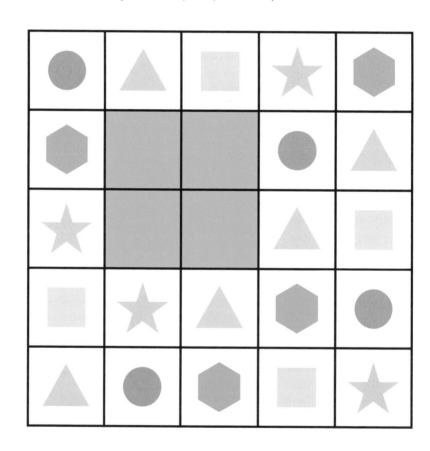

Puzzles and Brainteasers

EVERY TIME. EVERY HAND.

October 15th is Global Handwashing Day. Washing your hands is the best way to prevent any bacteria in your poo from getting in your food, eyes, or anywhere else it doesn't belong.

A

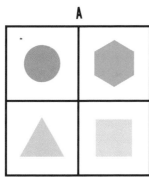

B

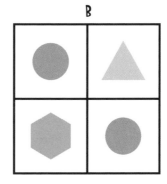

C

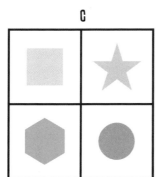

D

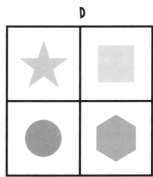

FUN FACT

Sloths climb down from their trees once a week to poo.

ANSWER ON PAGE 125

#52 SLANTED NUMBERS

The best poos are neat and round—not square. If you have a square poo, you may need to eat more fiber. Or stop eating blocks! You can also solve this puzzle to ease your pain. Write a number in each empty square so that every row and column contains all of the numbers from 1 to 6. Clues outside the grid show the total of all the numbers in the marked diagonals.

Example

	16	6	5	3	
	5	2	1	4	3	9
5	2	4	5	3	1	6
4	1	3	4	5	2	6
6	3	5	2	1	4	5
15	4	1	3	2	5	
	4	4	9	9		

Puzzles and Brainteasers

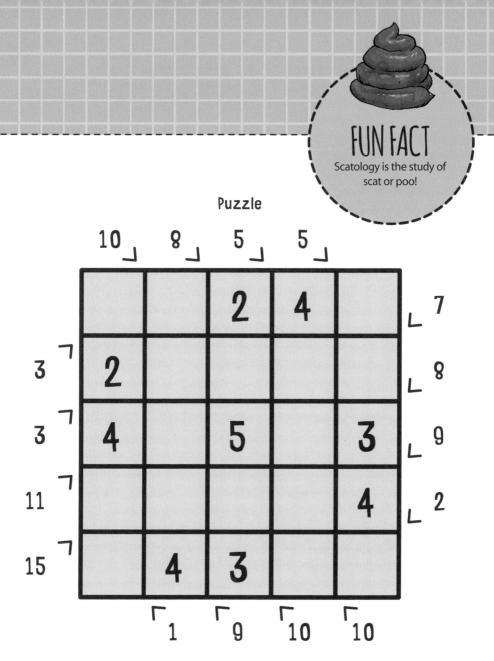

Puzzle

ANSWER ON PAGE 125

 # THE PSYCHOLOGY OF POO

Settled in the toilet, a creatively shaped poo can look like a Rorschach test, the ink marks that are used to understand how people think. What do you see in the shapes below? A wild party? A face? Just more poo? There are no wrong answers!

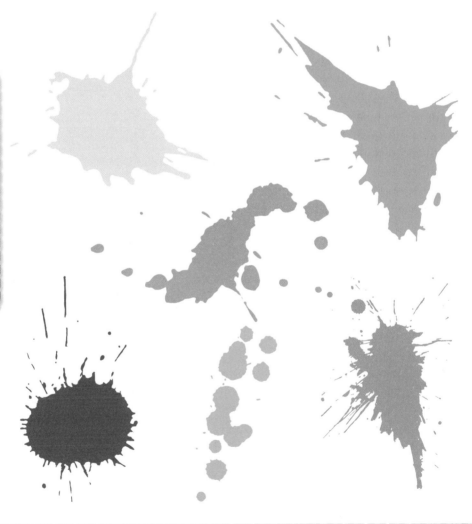

WHAT'S YOUR TP PERSONALITY?

When you visit a new bathroom, this is the kind of toilet paper you hope to find.

The Thicker the Better
You believe toilet paper is a wall between your hands and poo that should never be crossed.

Cheap like Paper
You don't want to spend any extra time or money in the bathroom.

Strong
Double ply is the only ply for the doo doo on your derriere.

Quilted
You seek warmth, comfort, and cleaning power in your roll.

FUN FACT
Astronauts have left behind more than one bag of poo on the moon.

KNICKER ART

Try this dot-to-dot with a twist. Draw lines to join all the dots that are in the 3-times table, starting at 3 and going all the way up to 174 in increasing numerical order. Remember, you should ignore any dot that's not in the 3-times table.

Puzzles and Brainteasers

#55 THE SUPER BOWL

Flash. Flesh. Flush. One little letter can make a big difference. How many words can you find in this toilet? Each word must use the *W*, plus at least two other letters. However, you can't use a letter more than once in any word. There is at least one word that uses all of the letters—see if you can find it!

ANSWERS ON PAGE 125

#56 MESSY MATH

It's normal to poo anywhere from three times a day to three times a week, but it's always good to keep your eye on the numbers. Place a number from 1 to 9 into each of the white squares, so that each continuous horizontal or vertical set of white squares adds up to the value given at its start. Avoid using a number more than once in any answer. (For example, you could make 4 by using 1+3 but not 2+2.)

Example

			7	14		
		15\20	**6**	**9**		
	7\17	**4**	**1**	**2**	10	10
17	**8**	**9**	19\23	**3**	**7**	**9**
24	**9**	**7**	**8**	3\17	**2**	**1**
		16	**6**	**9**	**1**	
		17	**9**	**8**		

FUN FACT
Now $3.5 million dollars less rich, Lam Sai-wing is the proud owner of the world's most expensive bathroom in the world!

Puzzle 1

Puzzle 2

ANSWERS ON PAGE 125

#57 LONELY LETTER

Staring at yourself in the mirror. Listening to the echo of your poo plopping into the toilet. Singing to yourself in the shower. It can get lonely in the bathroom. One of the letters in this activity is lonely too. Every letter appears twice, except for one that appears only once. Which letter is that?

B U Y Q R y R
E C W I N G D
X V C T H S
    M J B E
J Z L Q A
    K U D X
H O P
    G T
K A Z L S V
F F P W I M O

ANSWER ON PAGE 126

 EUREKA!

Some of history's most brilliant thinkers have had their greatest ideas lounging in the bathtub or taking a shower. Does spending time in the bathroom make you smarter? Probably not. But it can relax your brain enough to come up with a solution to a problem you've been thinking about for a while. Use this activity to get ready for your next Aha! moment. Which number comes next in each of the following math sequences?

Puzzle 1

128   64   32   16   8   4   _____?

Puzzle 2

2   5   9   14   20   27   _____?

Puzzle 3

2   3   5   8   13   21   _____?

FUN FACT
In a lifetime, the average person poos 25,000 times.
How many poos have you pooed?

#59 BATH TIME CHALLENGE

Rub a dub dub! Can you find the toy hidden in these tiles? To find it, you just have to shade in some tiles according to the rules.

Rules:
- There is a clue at the start of each row or column, made up of one or more numbers. This tells you how many touching squares in that row or column you should shade. For example, if the clue is 5 then you should shade five touching squares in that row, and leave the rest blank. (Hint: Put an X in the squares you know are blank.)
- If the clue has more than one number, there is more than one set of shaded squares in that row or column, which mustn't touch one another. For example, if the clue is 5, 2 then there are five shaded touching squares, at least one blank square, and then two shaded touching squares.
- The clues are given in order, so if the clue is 5, 2 then you know the five touching squares come before the two touching squares, reading left-to-right or top-to-bottom.

Puzzles and Brainteasers

FUN FACT

Rubber duckies have been keeping kids company in the bath since the 1940s.

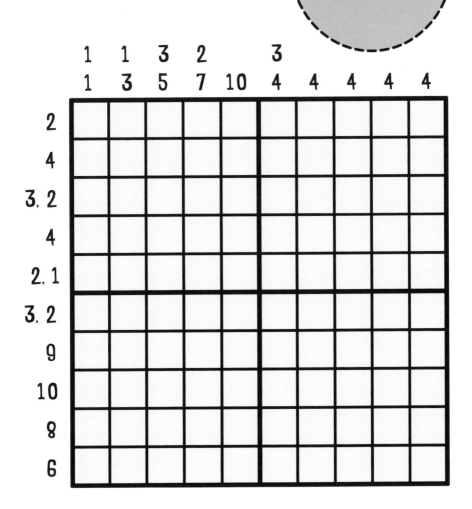

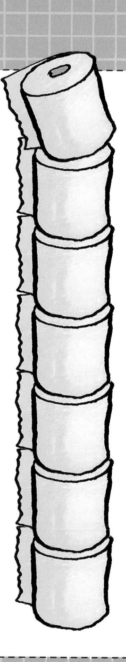

#60 THE LEANING TOWER OF TP

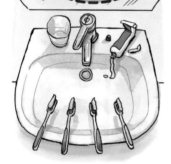

In 2015, a team of two people stacked 28 rolls of toilet paper in a soft, white tower, earning them a place in the Guinness Book of World Records. How many rolls of TP can you stack in 30 seconds?

DIRTY JOBS
Toothbrush, TP, or toilet…which do you think has the worst job in the bathroom?

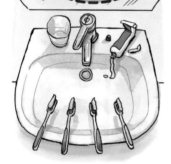

THE FIRST TP
Throughout history, hands and water were long the toilet paper of choice. Clay, stone, coconuts, shells, snow, moss, hay, newspapers, wool, corn cobs, and grass have all been used too. Makes even that see-through toilet paper look pretty good, doesn't it?

#61 WEIRD WORDS

Can you work out which is the odd word out from each of the following sets, and why?

Puzzle 1

| Crane | Digger | Car | Bulldozer |

Why: _____

Puzzle 2

| Robin | Bat | Man | Crane |

Why: _____

Puzzle 3

| Tales | Steal | Least | Seals |

Why: _____

FUN FACT Americans spend more than $6 billion a year on toilet paper.

ANSWERS ON PAGE 126

Sometimes you just know it's going to be a Two-Flush Poo, so you reach around back and press the handle before you're through. It's better for everyone: you, the next person in the bathroom, and the pipes. Practice turning each of these pictures by its corresponding arrow, and match it to the correct image below. Rotate Puzzle 1 by 90 degrees clockwise; rotate Puzzle 2 by 180 degrees; and rotate Puzzle 3 by 90 degrees counterclockwise.

Puzzles and Brainteasers

CAREFUL WHERE YOU STEP

The white beaches in the Caribbean are some of the most beautiful on Earth, but it's easier to appreciate how pretty they are if you don't know the white sand is made of parrotfish poo.

2

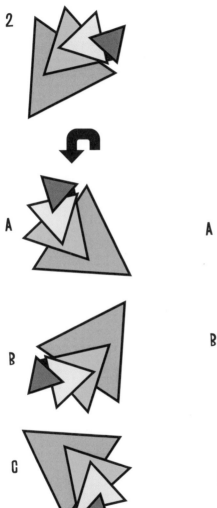

3

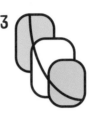

A

B

C

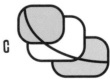

ANSWERS ON PAGE 126

#63 SHADOW MATCH

Hopefully you're not seeing stars when you poo! If you do, pay attention and tell someone. In the meantime, make sure you'll know a star when you see one—no matter which direction it's pointed. Which of these shadows matches the outline of the larger shape at the top of the page?

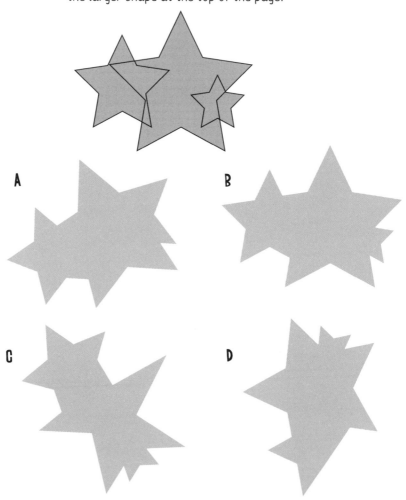

A

B

C

D

ANSWER ON PAGE 126

A FART IS A WISH YOUR BUTT MAKES

Tinkle, tinkle, down it goes.

Now I smell it in my nose.

In the water the doo doo lands

I'm just glad it's not in my hands.

FUN FACT

Mozart is famous for writing classical symphonies, but he also wrote more than his share of silly songs about poo in letters to friends and family. Mozart's poo obsession was so pronounced that the writer Stefan Zweig once sent his letters to Sigmund Freud to be psychoanalyzed.

MAXIMUM PEE SPEED

Each time you visit the bathroom, log the number of seconds it takes you to go. Look for patterns and review your results after a week.

Number 1	Number 2	Seconds
____	____	____
____	____	____
____	____	____
____	____	____
____	____	____
____	____	____
____	____	____
____	____	____

#64 JIGSAW POOZLE

A perfect poo is the result of several smaller pieces of poo joining together. Their shapes may vary, but together they form one large piece of poo that comes out clean and smooth. Celebrate this poo of interlocking genius with this activity. Draw along the dashed lines to divide each image into four identical shapes. While the shapes can be rotated relative to one another, none of them should be reflected. Each shape will be made up of five squares, and none of the shapes will overlap.

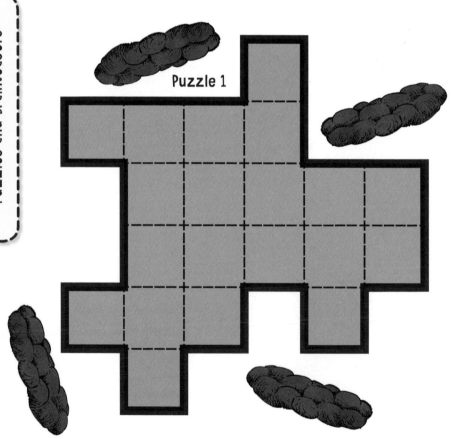

Puzzle 1

FUN FACT

Large piles of manure have burst into flames without warning. When the piles get wet, a chemical reaction causes the temperature to slowly rise until the poo ignites.

Puzzle 2

ANSWERS ON PAGE 126

#65 TAKING THE LONG WAY

Without enough fiber, poo can get long and skinny, like a pencil. When it comes out, it can feel like it's taking the least direct route possible. You can trace its path in the grid below. Fill in the empty squares so the grid on the next page contains every number from 1 to 36 just once. Start at 1, move on to 2, then 3, and so on by moving only to grid squares that touch. You can only move left, right, up, and down between squares, not diagonally.

the grid on the next page

Example

9	10	11	12	13	14
8	7	6	19	18	15
3	4	5	20	17	16
2	1	22	21	36	35
25	24	23	30	31	34
26	27	28	29	32	33

FUN FACT
Archaeologists have found pieces of human poo that are 50,000 years old!

Puzzles and Brainteasers

FLYING POO

Unlike human kidneys, which produce pee, bird kidneys produce a white paste. The white paste combines with the waste produced in the intestines to produce the white bird poo we see everywhere.

Puzzle

		21	20		
	25			16	
27		13	12		10
28		30	7		9
	34			5	
		32	1		

ANSWER ON PAGE 126

WHO DUNNIT?

Can you solve this bathroom mystery? Some of the empty squares in this puzzle contain piles of poo. Each numbered square tells you how many poo piles it is touching (including diagonal squares). Choose which squares have poo in them. None of the numbered squares contain poo.

	4		3		
	5		3	2	2
		1			1
	3	1	2		1
3	4			2	1
		3			

ANSWER ON PAGE 127

#67 FASHIONABLE FARTER

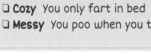

- ❏ **Proud** You love the smell of your own farts
- ❏ **Happy** You do a little dance after each fart
- ❏ **Shy** You keep your farts quiet and private
- ❏ **Smart** You know all the best places to let a fart fly
- ❏ **Athletic** You fart when you're running, jumping, or swimming
- ❏ **Cozy** You only fart in bed
- ❏ **Messy** You poo when you try to fart

Oh no! The smell is overpowering! Now part of the bathroom wallpaper has fallen off. Which of the options should be used to replace the shaded area in order to continue the existing pattern?

Puzzles and Brainteasers

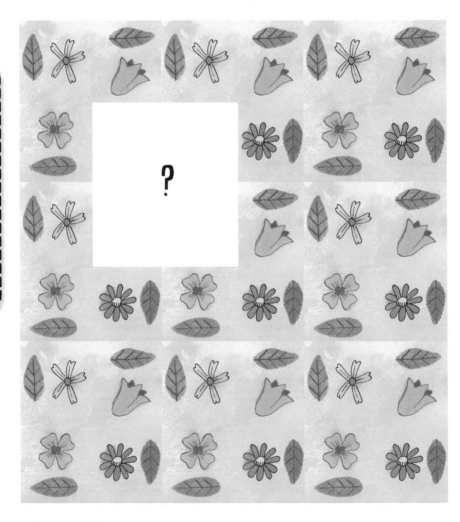

POO PAPER

Cow, elephant, moose, and donkey dung have all been used to make paper. Fortunately, it smells like paper not poo.

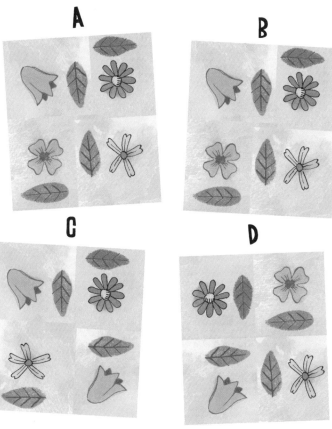

A

B

C

D

FUN FACT

Arctic penguins produce so much poo it can be seen from outer space!

ANSWER ON PAGE 127

FLOATING NUMBERS

2

Are you famous for your sinkers or your floaters? Or maybe you're famous for your stinkers! Add together two or more numbers to make each of the totals below. Each floating number can only be used once per total.

6
3
5
9
8

12   16   19   25

IF THESE PIPES COULD TALK

Plumbers have found mops, golf clubs, wood, carpet, and even a refrigerator down in the sewers.

The vowels have been flushed out of these words, which are all related in some way to school. Work out which vowels are missing from each word. The first one is done for you as an example.

1) MTH: MATH
2) FTBLL: _____
3) TCHRS: _____
4) CRYN: _____
5) DCTN: _____
6) RT: _____
7) RSR: _____
8) XM: _____
9) CCH: _____
10) FFCS: _____

DEEP THOUGHTS

"To pee, or not to pee (in the shower), that is the question." –The Bard of the Bathroom, aka Shakespeare. A quote loosely based on "To be, or not to be, that is the question" from *Hamlet*.

#71 DOO DOO DOMINOES

The bathroom might just be the perfect place to play a peaceful game of dominoes. It's you, the dominoes, and a little poo. There's plenty of time. And no one will know if you cheat! Each of the loose dominoes at the bottom of the opposite page fits into one of the shaded domino positions. Use your pencil to draw the dots on the shaded dominoes, crossing out the loose dominoes as you use them. Just like the two dominoes that are already placed in the bottom corner, the halves of the dominoes that are facing each other should contain the same number of dots.

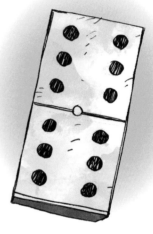

FUN FACT

When whales dive down to catch their dinner, the tremendous pressure of the water above them stops their digestion so they can only poo when they are back at the surface!

110

FRESH AS A FLOWER

You can make your own room deodorizer with an adult's help. Grab a spray bottle and mix a tablespoon of essential oils that smell good, vegetable glycerin, and rubbing alcohol in a cup of water. Spray into the bowl each time you let a smelly poo loose.

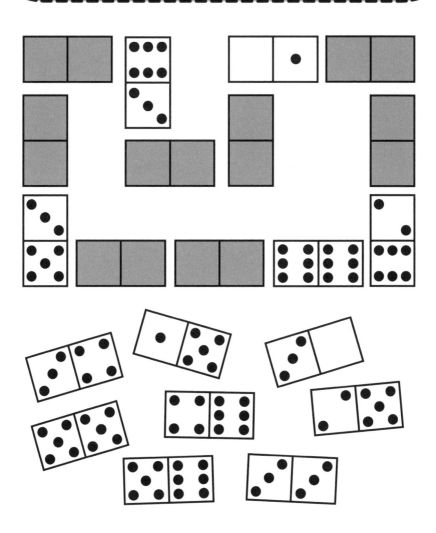

ANSWER ON PAGE 127

#72 WATCH IT!

Talking about poo is all fun and games until you find yourself face to face with poo outside the bathroom. Nobody wants that. Look at this drawing of a park. There are four people, four dogs, and four piles of dog poo. To clean up this mess, draw two straight lines, each one starting on one edge and running across to the other edge, to divide the park into four separate areas. These lines can be in any direction, but each area must contain exactly one person, one dog, and one poo.

ANSWER ON PAGE 127

PIC-PAC-POO

If tic-tac-toe is feeling old, try the bathroom version: Pic-Pac-Poo! It's about as different as it sounds. Place an X or an O into every empty square of this grid, without making any horizontal, vertical or diagonal lines of four or more Xs or Os.

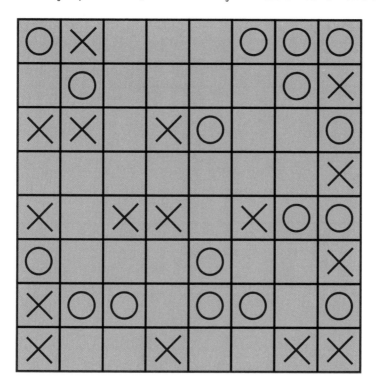

OH POO!

The word *poo* can be used as a verb, noun, and even an exclamation. It was first used in the 16th century, became popular in the 1800s, and it's still just as fun to say today!

ANSWER ON PAGE 127

 # PAPER ROUTE

In this picture, each of the dots represents a poo, and the lines are rolls of toilet paper stretched between each mess. It's your job to connect all the poos in one single loop of toilet paper. This means every poo must have exactly two pieces of toilet paper connected to it. Toilet paper can only be placed horizontally or vertically, and not in any diagonal direction.

Puzzles and Brainteasers

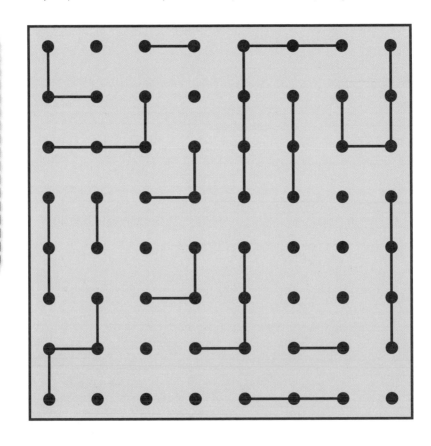

ANSWER ON PAGE 128

SPLISH SPLASH

What sound does your poo make?

Silent Your poo sessions are as quiet as an Olympic diver entering the pool

Gassy Your poo is mixed with toots

Natural Your poo hits the water like rain boots in a puddle

FUN FACT

Drivers in Britain can buy cars powered by human poo!

#75 THE GREAT PYRAMID

To build a pyramid that will stand the test of time and be admired by bathroom tourists around the world for millennia to come, fill in all the empty tissue boxes in this pyramid. Each box should contain a value that's equal to the sum of the two boxes immediately below it. For example, notice how the 4 and I in the bottom row add up to the 5 in the box directly above them.

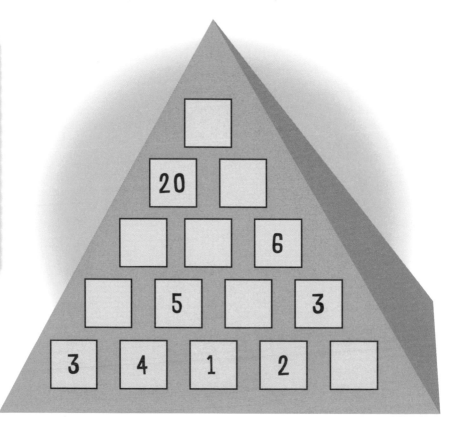

FOODS THAT HELP YOU POO

Feeling a little stuffed up? Try one of these foods. Although really anything with fiber in it can get your poo moving so you feel like new!

Beans

Popcorn

Whole-grain bread

Potatoes

Apricots

Prunes

Broccoli

Nuts

#76 THAT SHIP HAS SAILED

Can you find the bath toy hidden in these tiles? To find it, shade
in the tiles according to the rules.

Rules:
- There is a clue at the start of each row or column, made up of one or more numbers. This tells you how many touching squares in that row or column you should shade. For example, if the clue is 5 then you should shade five touching squares in that row, and leave the rest blank. (Hint: Put an X in the squares you know are blank.)
- If the clue has more than one number, there is more than one set of shaded squares in that row or column, which mustn't touch one another. For example, if the clue is 5, 2 then there are five shaded touching squares, at least one blank square, and then two shaded touching squares.
- The clues are given in order, so if the clue is 5, 2 then you know the five touching squares come before the two touching squares, reading left-to-right or top-to-bottom.

	1	2	3	4	5					
	1	2	3	3	3	10	3	3	2	1
1										
2										
3										
4										
5										
6										
1										
10										
8										
6										

ANSWER ON PAGE 128

#77 DOCTOR'S ORDERS

It's all fun and games until someone poos a poo that should never be pooed. Every so often everyone has poo troubles. But that's what doctors are for. (Best job in the world, right?) Tell them your poo woes, and they'll help you feel healthy, happy, and ready to poo with the best of them. So next time you're not feeling well in the poo department, tell your doctor. And while you mend, you can find words in this word square. Start on any letter and then move to neighboring letters, including those on a diagonal, without revisiting a square. For example, if you start on the *M* you could move to one of the *A*s and then to the *T* to make "MAT." There is one twelve-letter word that uses every square.

(Hint: it's something you might be given at the doctor's office.)

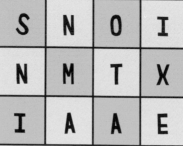

S	N	O	I
N	M	T	X
I	A	A	E

_____

_____

_____

_____

_____

_____

_____

ANSWERS ON PAGE 128

1. Bathroom Detective

Answer: A is missing a piece of string. B is missing a piece of chalk. C is missing the screws on the bottom of the toilet. D is missing a pink ball.

2. Toot, Toot!
Answer:

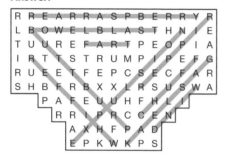

3. Magic Number Twos
Answer:

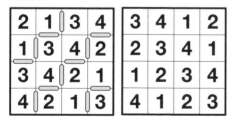

4. Toilet Paper Chains
Possible answers:

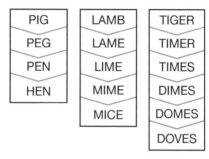

PIG	LAMB	TIGER
PEG	LAME	TIMER
PEN	LIME	TIMES
HEN	MIME	DIMES
	MICE	DOMES
		DOVES

5. Great Poo Mountain
Answer:

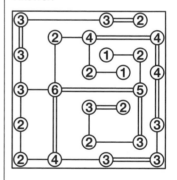

6. Out of Order
Answer: The circle is the heaviest; the square is the lightest.

7. Poo Pennies
Answer: 1. 3 coins = 5 + 2 + 2; **2.** 4 coins = 50 + 20 + 2 + 1; **3.** 3 coins = 27 cents in change, made up of 20 + 5 + 2; **4.** 7 coins = 10 + 10 + 5 + 5 + 2 + 2 + 1

8. Target Practice

Answer: $14 = 3 + 5 + 6$; $21 = 8 + 5 + 8$; $23 = 6 + 6 + 11$; $28 = 15 + 5 + 8$

9. Caught Short

Answer:

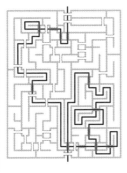

10. Dirty Laundry

Answer: A/H, B/G, C/F, D/E

11. The Toothbrush Test

Answer: 1. David; 2. Beatrice; 3. Abigail; 4. Charlotte

15. Plumbing Problem

Answer: 1/C, 2/A, 3/B

17. Hiya, Neighbor

Answer:

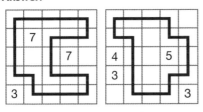

18. Battleship

Answer:

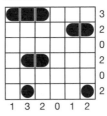

19. Backups For Your Bum

Answer: Puzzle 1 = 12 boxes; Puzzle 2 = 30 boxes

20. Counting Tiles

Answer:

Puzzle 1

2	4	6			2
		6			
	6				
4				2	4

Puzzle 2

4			3		
					4
	2	3	4		
		4	3	3	
3					
		2			1

21. Wiz Kid

Answer:

1	8	4	6	2	5	7	3
3	2	5	7	4	1	8	6
6	3	2	5	8	7	4	1
8	7	1	4	6	3	5	2
5	4	6	2	1	8	3	7
7	1	3	8	5	6	2	4
2	6	8	3	7	4	1	5
4	5	7	1	3	2	6	8

24. Doodie Doodles

Answer: A/F; B/G; C/H; D/E

25. Pop-Up Porta Potty
Answer:

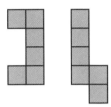

26. Loose Vowels
Answer: Toothbrush; Shower; Towel; Toilet; Comb; Faucet

27. Dirty Dominoes
Answer:

	6	1		2	2	3	
	3	3	6	6	6	3	4
1	4	5	5	5	2	5	3
1	5		1	1	2	3	4
5	1	2	4	6		4	4
6	2	6		5	1	5	4
2	6	1		3	2	4	3

28. Crisscross Cotton Swabs

Puzzle 1

Puzzle 2

Answer: Puzzle 1 = 4 small squares and 1 large square; Puzzle 2 = 9 small squares, 4 medium squares, and 1 large square

29. Artsy TP
Answer: 7 hexagons; 4 pentagons

31. Reflections
Answer: 1. B; 2. C; 3. B

32. Bathroom Bother
Answer: Skull missing from gas; crossbones missing from gas; arrow through the heart graffiti missing from first stall; zipper on backpack missing from first stall; smiley face graffiti missing from second stall; ruler in backpack missing from second stall; "Benny B." graffiti missing from third stall; stick figure with thought bubble missing from third stall; door knob missing from fourth stall; laces on left shoe missing from fourth stall.

33. Chocolate Log-Doku
Answer:

B	E	A	D	C
D	A	C	E	B
C	B	E	A	D
A	C	D	B	E
E	D	B	C	A

34. In and Out
Answer:

35. Control the Flow
Answer: Puzzle 1 = x3; Puzzle 2 = x2, +1

37. Roman Relations
Answer:

3 ˅	2	6 ˟	4	5	1
4 ˅	1	5	3	6	2
2	6 ˟	4 ˅	1	3	5
1	5	3	2	4 ˟	6
5	3 ˅	2	6	1 ˅	4
6 ˟	4 ˅	1	5	2 ˅	3

39. Bigger or Smaller
Answer:

Puzzle 1

2	1	4	3
1	2 <	3 <	4
3	4	2	1
4 >	3	1	2

Puzzle 2

2	4	1	3
1	3 <	4	2
4	2	3	1
3	1	2	4

42. What Am I?
Answer: Toilet paper

44. P.U.
Answer:

E	F	D	A	C	B
B	A	C	E	D	F
D	E	F	B	A	C
C	B	A	D	F	E
F	D	E	C	B	A
A	C	B	F	E	D

45. Exit Plan
Answer: Puzzle 1 = 9 squares, plus an additional 20 rectangles; Puzzle 2 = 14 squares, plus an additional 26 rectangles.

46. Don't Break the Chain
Answer:

20	19	24	12	6	26

13	52	48	61	45	50

20	4	44	40	50	25

47. Potty Training
Answer:

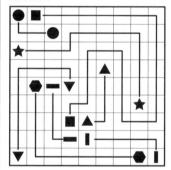

48. Tricky Turds
Answer: 2 pairs = A4/C3; B3/C4

49. Odd Shape Out
Answer: 4, because it is the only shape with 7 sides when all others have 6

50. Poodoku
Answer:

2	3	1	💩	5	4
5	4	💩	1	3	2
4	1	3	5	2	💩
💩	5	2	4	1	3
3	💩	5	2	4	1
1	2	4	3	💩	5

51. Potty Patterns
Answer: C (No shape repeats in either row or column.)

52. Slanted Numbers
Answer:

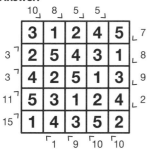

10, 8, 5, 5

3	1	2	4	5	7
2	5	4	3	1	8
4	2	5	1	3	9
5	3	1	2	4	2
1	4	3	5	2	

3, 3, 11, 15 (left)
1, 9, 10, 10 (bottom)

54. Knicker Art
Answer:

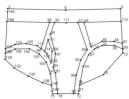

55. The Super Bowl
Answer: Two words use all the letters: *wonderful* or *underflow*; other words are *dew, dowel, down, drew, drown, endow, few, flew, flow, flowed, flower, flown, fowl, fowled, frown, frowned, lewd, low, lowed, lower, new, now, owe, owed, owl, own, owned, owner, row, rowed, rowel, unwed, wed, weld, wen, wend, woe, woeful, wolf, wolfed, won, wonder, word, wore, world, worn, would, wound, wounder, wren*

56. Messy Math
Answer:
Puzzle 1

1	3		2	1
2	7	1	3	2
2	3	8		
2	9	7		
2	3	1	3	9
1	2		1	2

Puzzle 2

1	3		
1	3	2	4
7	9	2	1
9	8	9	5
2	7	3	1
9	5		

57. Lonely Letter
Answer: N

58. Eureka!
Answer: Puzzle 1 = 2 (the number halves at each step); Puzzle 2 = 35 (the difference between numbers increases by 1 at each step); Puzzle 3 = 34 (the previous two numbers are added together at each step)

59. Bath Time Challenge
Answer:

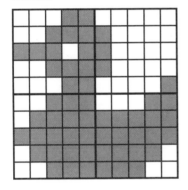

61. Weird Words
Answer: Puzzle 1 = Car (all others are vehicles you'd find on a construction site); Puzzle 2 = Man (all others are animals that can fly); Puzzle 3 = Seals (all others are anagrams of the letters A, E, L, S, and T)

62. Rotating on Your Axis
Answer: 1. C; 2. B; 3. A

63. Shadow Match
Answer: B

64. Jigsaw Poozle
Answer:
Puzzle 1

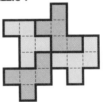

Puzzle 2

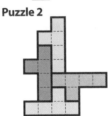

65. Taking the Long Way
Answer:

23	22	21	20	19	18
24	25	14	15	16	17
27	26	13	12	11	10
28	29	30	7	8	9
35	34	31	6	5	4
36	33	32	1	2	3

66. Who Dunnit?
Answer:

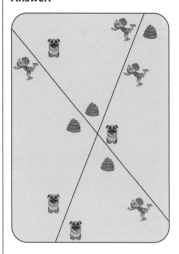

68. Wallpaper Whoopsie
Answer: D

69. Floating Numbers
Answer: $12 = 9 + 3$; $16 = 8 + 5 + 3$; $19 = 8 + 6 + 5$; $25 = 9 + 8 + 5 + 3$

70. Flushed Away Vowels
Answer: Math; Football; Teachers; Crayon; Education (or Diction); Art (or Ratio or Rote); Eraser; Exam; Coach; Offices

71. Doo Doo Dominoes
Answer:

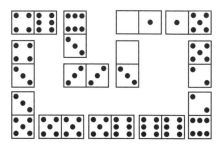

72. Watch It!
Answer:

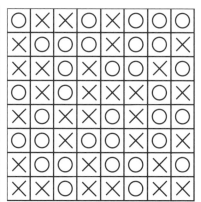

73. Pic-Pac-Poo
Answer:

O	X	X	O	X	O	O	O
X	O	O	O	X	O	O	X
X	X	O	X	O	O	X	O
O	X	O	X	X	O	X	X
X	O	X	O	X	O	X	O
O	O	X	O	O	X	O	X
X	O	O	X	O	O	X	O
X	X	X	O	X	O	X	X

74. Paper Route
Answer:

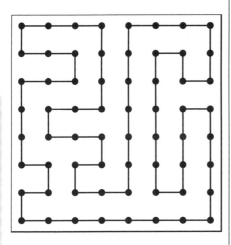

75. The Great Pyramid
Answer:

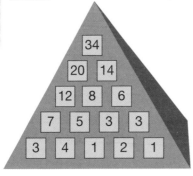

76. That Ship Has Sailed
Answer:

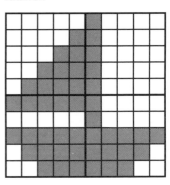

77. Doctor's Orders
Answer: Twelve-letter word is *examinations*. The other words are *aim, aims, animate, animation, animations, ate, atom, atoms, axe, axiom, axioms, axon, axons, eat, eta, exam, examination, examinations, exams, exit, inmate, inn, inns, ins, ion, ions, iota, main, mains, man, mans, mat, mate, mote, nation, nations, nominate, not, note, smote, tam, tams, tan, tans, tax, taxi, tea, team, teams, tom, toms, ton, tons*

Puzzles and Brainteasers

CRAFTS

By now, you have mastered more than 70 brainteasers,
which means you're probably going through toilet paper
like crazy. But there's no need to toss out those empty
rolls with the trash. This section will show you how to
transform an ordinary piece of cardboard into TP versions
of Hello Kitty, Minions, and more. Roll with the artsy crowd
and craft your own bathroom cheering squad. You can even
make a confetti popper to celebrate an extra big poo!

IMPORTANT
Whenever a craft calls for hot glue or a
craft knife—or you just want to make a
project more fun—ask an adult for help!

GOING PRO
Even professional Parisian artists have found themselves
inspired by a spare roll of TP. Artist Anastassia Elias creates
delicate dioramas inside the rolls. You can see her work in
her book, *Rouleaux*, which means "rolls" in French.

#78 BINOCULARS

Supplies needed

- scissors
- scrapbook paper
- 2 toilet-paper rolls
- hot glue
- washi tape
- clothespin
- ribbon

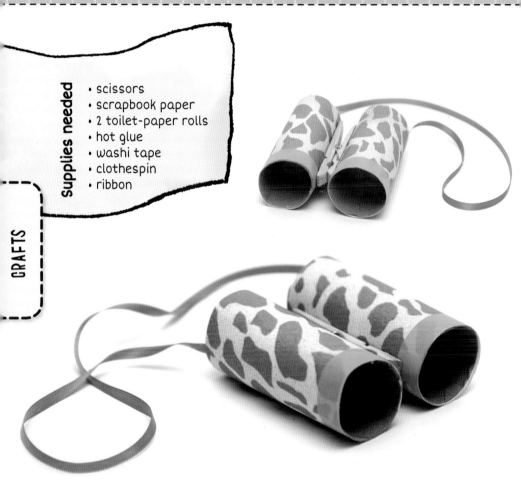

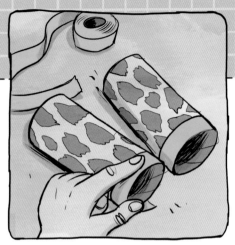

STEP ONE
Cut two pieces of scrapbook paper to the size of your toilet-paper rolls. Glue into place.

STEP TWO
Add washi tape around the edge of the toilet-paper roll.

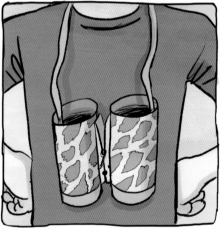

STEP THREE
Glue a clothespin to connect the two rolls.

STEP FOUR
To create a strap, glue a long ribbon to the inside of each roll. Now let's get out of this smelly bathroom and explore!

#79 SUPERHERO CUFFS

Supplies needed
- scissors
- toilet-paper roll
- white paint
- paintbrush
- washi tape
- hole punch
- ribbon

STEP ONE

Feel like your poos are super human? Cut the toilet-paper roll in half, and then cut each piece open. Next paint the inside and outside of your toilet-paper roll.

STEP TWO

Pick out some fun washi tape, and press it firmly onto the armband.

STEP THREE

Finally, use a hole punch to make a hole on each side of the cuffs and add a matching ribbon to keep your cuffs in place. Poo power!

#80 BIRD FEEDER

CRAFTS

Supplies needed

- scissors
- yellow construction paper
- toilet-paper roll
- hot glue
- ruler
- hole punch
- paper straws
- ribbon
- peanut butter
- birdseed

STEP ONE

Cut a piece of construction paper to the size of the toilet-paper roll, and glue it onto your roll.

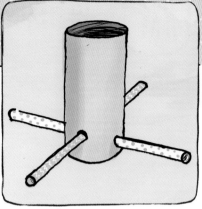

STEP TWO

Use a hole punch to make two holes 1 inch from the bottom and two holes ½ inch higher on the other sides. Feed the straws through the holes to form an X.

STEP THREE

Punch two more holes at the top of the roll. Add some bright ribbon so you can hang the bird feeder in a tree.

STEP FOUR

Spread peanut butter on the top half of the feeder and sprinkle birdseed on top. Feeding the birds is an activity generations have enjoyed—before or after a good poo.

#81 SNAKE

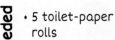

Supplies needed

- 5 toilet-paper rolls
- light and dark green paint
- paintbrush
- scissors
- ruler
- green pipe cleaner
- googly eyes
- hot glue
- black ribbon

STEP ONE

Paint your toilet-paper rolls dark green on one side and light green on the other.

STEP TWO

Collapse each roll and cut the ends into points. Except at the front of the head and end of the tail, use your hole punch to make a hole at the end of each roll.

STEP THREE

Cut the pipe cleaner into pieces that are each 1½ inches long. Connect the body pieces by looping pipe cleaners through the two holes on each side and twisting at the bottom.

STEP FOUR

Glue googly eyes to the head. Cut a small piece of ribbon for your snake's tongue, and glue it into place. This snake is ready to slither. Don't be surprised if you find it peeking out of your toilet one day!

#82 NIGHTLIGHT

CRAFTS

Supplies needed

- white glue
- toilet-paper roll
- glitter
- scissors
- white construction paper
- watercolor paints
- paintbrush
- hot glue
- hole punch
- flameless tea light candle

STEP ONE

Spread a thin layer of glue on the inside of the toilet-paper roll, and sprinkle glitter inside.

STEP TWO

Cut a piece of white paper to fit the toilet-paper roll, and secure it with hot glue. Paint a design. It can be inspired by anything from the poo in your toilet to the art in your bedroom!

STEP THREE

Use a hole punch to make holes at the top and bottom of the nightlight. Add the flameless tea light to the bottom. Sweet dreams, TP Artists!

#83 CONFETTI POPPERS

Supplies needed

- paint
- paintbrush
- toilet-paper roll
- balloon
- scissors
- decorative duct tape
- construction paper

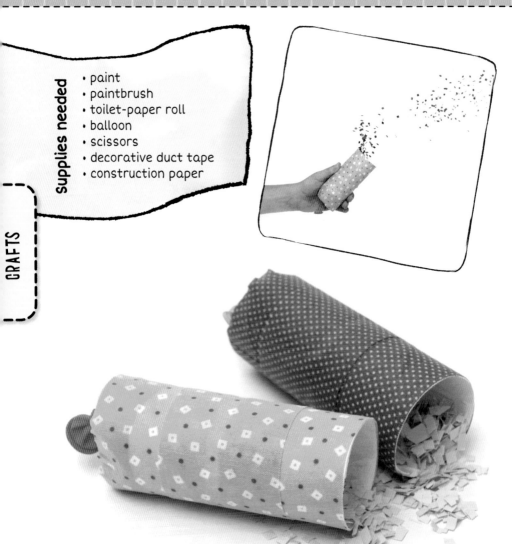

STEP ONE

Ready to throw a poo party? Start by painting the inside and outside of the toilet-paper roll. Let the paint dry 10 minutes. Tie the balloon at the end, and then cut it in half.

STEP TWO

Wrap the end of the balloon around the toilet-paper roll. Cut the tape into three pieces. Wrap one piece around the top, being sure to secure the balloon. Tape another piece to the bottom of the roll.

STEP THREE

Wrap the last piece of tape around the middle. Cut some small pieces of paper, and add them to the inside of your popper. Then throw them up in the air like you just don't care!

#84 BOWLING PINS

Supplies needed

- 6 toilet-paper rolls
- scissors
- white card stock or white paint
- hot glue
- red card stock
- star punch (optional)
- foam ball
- black paint
- paintbrush

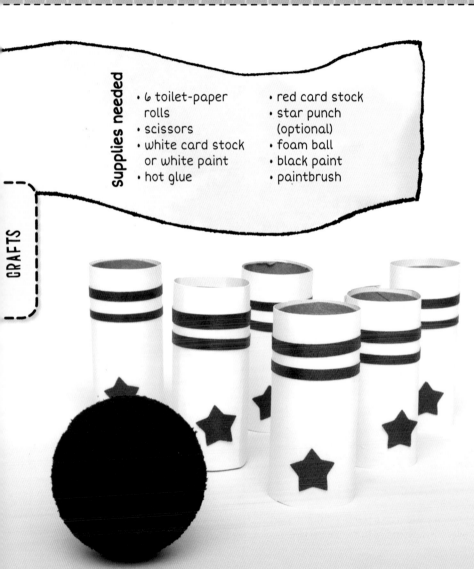

STEP ONE

Start by cutting white card stock to glue around each toilet-paper roll, or simply paint the rolls with white paint.

STEP TWO

Cut two thin strips of red card stock, and wrap them around the top of each roll.

STEP THREE

Cut 6 stars (or use a star punch), and glue them to the bottom of each roll.

STEP FOUR

Paint a medium foam ball with black paint. Once it dries, you're ready for some Bathroom Bowling!

#85 WIND CHIMES

supplies needed

- 3 toilet-paper rolls
- pencil with eraser
- paint
- paintbrush
- wooden skewer
- hole punch
- 9 bells
- ribbon
- twine

STEP ONE

Paint all three toilet-paper rolls different colors. Once they're dry, dip a pencil eraser in paint, and press the eraser onto the rolls to create polka dots.

STEP TWO

Paint the skewer to match. Punch holes through the top of each roll, making sure all the holes are at the same height. Once the paint has dried, push the skewer through.

STEP THREE

Cut three strips of twine, and tie three bells on each strip. Tie the strings to the skewer inside each toilet-paper roll. Tie a ribbon to each end of the wooden skewer. Tinkle, tinkle. I hear a happy pee song!

#86 ROCKET SHIP

supplies needed

- scissors
- construction paper
- toilet-paper roll
- craft glue
- reflective paper
- buttons

STEP ONE

Cut a piece of white paper a little longer than the toilet-paper roll, and glue it into place. Cut two strips of paper, and glue them around the toilet-paper roll.

STEP TWO

Cut a large circle for the top of the rocket. Cut a slit to the middle, and slide the two edges together to create a cone shape. Glue into place, and add to the top of the rocket ship.

STEP THREE

Cut a large triangle of yellow paper and a smaller triangle of orange paper for the flames. Cut two slits on the bottom on your rocket ship, and insert the triangles.

STEP FOUR

Use reflective paper (or another color) to make a circle for the window, and glue it to the front of the rocket ship. Add some buttons to finish the look. Blast off to Planet Poo!

#87 FUN MONSTERS

Supplies needed

- decorative scissors
- card stock
- toilet-paper roll
- hot glue
- paint
- thin paintbrush

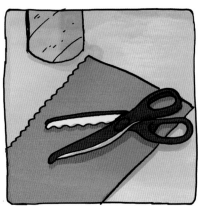

STEP ONE

Start by cutting a piece of card stock and gluing it around your toilet-paper roll. Use decorative scissors to create a wavy edge.

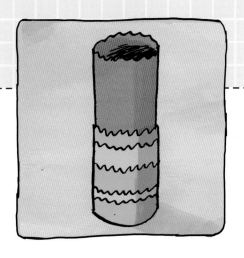

STEP TWO

Cut several thin strips of different colored card stock, and glue them around the bottom of the toilet-paper roll.

STEP THREE

Use your scissors to add some cool hair at the top.

STEP FOUR

Paint a face. Add as many fun details as you want. Just like there's no wrong way to poo, there's no wrong way to make these crazy bathroom creatures!

#88 OWLS

Supplies needed

- paint
- paintbrush
- toilet-paper roll
- construction paper
- scrapbook paper
- scissors
- circle punch
- craft glue
- hole punch

STEP ONE

Paint the toilet-paper roll with a bright color. Use two coats, and let each coat dry for at least 10 minutes. Once the paint is dry, fold over the top of the toilet-paper roll to create the top of the owl's head.

STEP TWO

Cut feathers out of scrapbook paper using a circle punch or by tracing out small circles. Trace the feet and beak, and cut out a small triangle for the beak and a heart for the feet.

STEP THREE

Glue the heart upside-down at the bottom to create feet. Glue the circles on in layers, and attach the beak. Fold a piece of paper in half and cut out an oval shape, leaving the ends a little pointy. Glue the wings on each side of the owl.

STEP FOUR

Cut large white circles for the eyes and small black circles for the pupils. Use a hole punch to make a small circle in the center of each. Glue the eyes on the owl. Isn't pooing a hoot?

#89 BUTTERFLIES

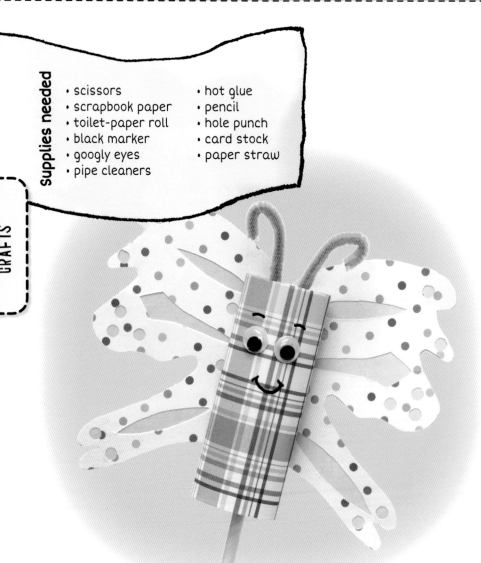

Supplies needed

- scissors
- scrapbook paper
- toilet-paper roll
- black marker
- googly eyes
- pipe cleaners
- hot glue
- pencil
- hole punch
- card stock
- paper straw

STEP ONE

Cut a piece of scrapbook paper and glue it around your toilet-paper roll. Glue on the eyes and draw a mouth. Cut the pipe cleaner into two short pieces. Attach them to the inside of the roll to create antennae.

STEP TWO

Fold a piece of paper in half, and use a pencil to draw one side of the wings along the fold. Cut along the outline to create a set of wings.

STEP THREE

Fold the wings over and cut out pieces (just like a paper snowflake). Use a hole punch to add some extra details.

STEP FOUR

Glue the wings to a solid piece of card stock and cut them out. Glue the center of the wings to the body. Attach a paper straw to the inside. This bathroom friend is ready to fly!

HYACINTHS

CRAFTS

Supplies needed

- scissors
- 2 toilet-paper rolls
- paint
- paintbrush
- green paper straws

- hot glue
- foam
- ribbon
- pom-pom balls

STEP ONE

Cut one toilet-paper roll in half, and press each piece flat. Paint both sides your favorite color. Let the paint dry, and then cut the cardboard into strips.

STEP TWO
Wrap each strip around the end of a paintbrush to create a curly fringe.

STEP THREE
Add a small dot of hot glue to the top of the straw. Glue the fringe around the straw to create the flower.

STEP FOUR
Cut your second toilet-paper roll in two (making one piece a little smaller). Paint the smaller half a pretty color for your pot, and add a little foam inside to keep the flower in place. Cut the larger half into leaves, painting them green. Cut 2 inches off the bottom of the straw, and firmly press it into the foam. Add pom-poms for grass. Glue the leaves to the stem. Add a small bow. Your bathroom still might smell like poo, but it will definitely be prettier now!

#91 HELLO KITTY

CRAFTS

Supplies needed

- white, black, and yellow paint
- paintbrush
- toilet-paper roll
- white glue
- yellow and pink glitter
- bow-tie noodle
- hot glue

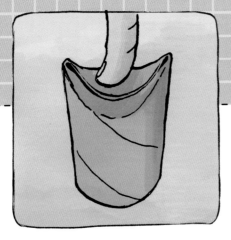

STEP ONE

Paint two layers of white paint over the toilet-paper roll. Let it dry for 10 minutes. Then fold over the top to create ears.

STEP TWO

Paint the eyes, nose, and whiskers. Add a thin coat of white glue to the nose, and sprinkle yellow glitter to make the nose sparkle. Then outline it with more black paint.

STEP THREE

Cover your bow-tie noodle in glue, and gently sprinkle the glitter over the top. Let the bow dry for at least 10 minutes.

STEP FOUR

Once the bow is dry, add a dot of hot glue to the back, and firmly press it onto the front of your kitty's ear. Meow!

#92 TMNT FINGER PUPPETS

Supplies needed

- scissors
- ruler
- 2 toilet-paper rolls
- yellow and green paint
- paintbrush
- clothespin
- craft glue
- construction paper
- black marker
- googly eyes

STEP ONE

Cut ½ inch off the top of one toilet-paper roll. (Save that part for the top of the turtle's head.) Then cut off all four corners to create the shell.

CRAFTS

STEP TWO

Paint the front of the shell yellow and the back and inside green. Then use a black marker to draw in the shell details on the chest and back.

STEP THREE

Cut open the second roll, and tighten the body so it's smaller than the shell. Glue and secure with a clothespin. Let it dry 15 to 20 minutes. Once it's dry, paint the body and the extra piece from step 1 green. This is the top of the head.

STEP FOUR

Cut two long strips and a circle out of brown paper. Cut one strip into two tassels for the belt. Write the turtle's initial on the circle. Cut a colored strip and tassels for the mask. Draw on the creases. Glue the turtle's body inside the shell, and glue the top of the head inside the body.

STEP FIVE

Wrap the belt around the turtle's shell, and glue it in place, along with the belt tassel and initial. Glue the mask around the top of the turtle's head. Finally, glue the mask tassel to the back of the mask.

STEP SIX

Draw the turtle's nose and mouth. Then add googly eyes with a little glue. Cowabunga, Poo Dudes!

#93 MINIONS

Supplies needed

- toilet-paper roll
- scissors
- tissue paper
- foam ball
- yellow, blue, black, and white paint
- paintbrush
- black fine-tip marker
- black and gray construction paper
- craft glue
- googly eyes

STEP ONE
Cut the toilet-paper roll to the height you want. Wrap some tissue paper around a small foam ball, and place it inside the roll.

STEP TWO
Add two coats of yellow paint over everything, and let it dry for 20 minutes. Paint the Minion's overalls in blue. Once the paint is dry, use a fine-tip black marker to add the stitches.

STEP THREE
Cut a long black strip of construction paper, and glue it around the Minion's head. Then cut two gray circles that are a little larger than the googly eyes, and glue the eyes on top. Attach the eyes to the Minion.

STEP FOUR
Finally, add the Minion's smile with black paint or marker. Use white paint for the teeth. Poo ba-boy bi-do! (That means "Poo on," in Minion.)

#94 BATMAN

Supplies needed

- scissors
- ruler
- gray, blue, white, beige, yellow, and black construction paper
- toilet-paper roll
- hot glue
- black fine-tip marker

STEP ONE

Cut a piece of gray paper to fit your toilet-paper roll. For the mask, cut a piece of blue paper about 2 inches tall and long enough to wrap around the toilet-paper roll. Remember the bat ears at the top. Cut out white eyes and a beige face.

STEP TWO

Glue the gray paper around the toilet paper roll, and add the mask on the top. Glue on the eyes and face. Draw a mouth.

STEP THREE

Cut a long strip of yellow paper, and draw on the gadgets with a fine-tip black marker. Use some blue paper for the briefs.

STEP FOUR

Trace the Batman symbol on black paper and cut it out. Place the symbol on yellow paper, and draw an oval around it. Cut out the oval, and glue the symbol to it. Glue the emblem to his chest. Draw a trapezoid on blue paper, and glue the cape to his back. Messy poo? Bathroom Batman to the rescue!

#95 RACE CAR

Supplies needed

- paint
- paintbrush
- toilet-paper roll
- scissors
- white, black, and gray construction paper
- fine-tip black marker
- hot glue
- hole punch
- paper fasteners

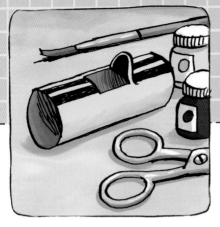

STEP ONE

Paint the toilet-paper roll inside and out. Let it dry for 20 minutes. Then, cut an opening at the top, and paint the seat. Cut away the excess around the seat. Paint a decorative stripe on the car.

STEP TWO

Cut a circle of white paper for the steering wheel. Use a marker to draw details. Glue the steering wheel on the car at an angle. Flatten the bottom of the car. Punch two holes for the wheels.

STEP THREE

Cut black circles for the wheels and smaller gray circles for the rims, and glue them together. Make a small hole in the middle of the wheel, and give the rims some detail with the marker. Push the paper fasteners through the wheels, and attach them to the race car.

STEP FOUR

Use the marker to draw doors. Cut two slits on the back of the car and bend to create your spoiler. Cut a small trapezoid of black paper, and glue it into place to finish the spoiler. Ready. Set. Poo!

#96 TIGER

Supplies needed

- orange card stock
- scissors
- toilet-paper roll
- black marker
- hot glue
- craft knife
- ruler
- orange and black pipe cleaners

STEP ONE

Cut the orange paper to the size of the toilet paper roll, and add tiger stripes with black marker. Glue the paper around the roll, and let it dry. Ask an adult to use a craft knife to cut a 2-inch slit at the top and bottom of one side. This is where you will insert the tiger's legs.

STEP TWO

Trace and cut out the tiger's legs. Repeat on another piece of card stock and glue the two pieces together to make the legs firm. Do the same for the back legs. Then draw the tiger's stripes with black marker.

STEP THREE

Bend the legs to make the tiger look like its is walking. Gently insert the front legs into the first slit on the roll. For the back legs, make a small hole in the center (for the tail), and insert the legs in the second slit. Twist an orange and a black pipe cleaner together for the tail, and push them through the small hole in the back legs.

STEP FOUR

Draw the shape of the head. Add eyes, a nose, a mouth, and stripes on the face. Cut out the head and a small tab for the neck. Bend and glue the tab to the back of the head. Then, attach it to the body. This tiger makes the purr-fect toy for the bathroom!

Supplies needed

- scissors
- ruler
- toilet-paper roll
- white construction paper
- craft glue
- hole punch
- wooden skewer
- foam ball
- pencil
- tinfoil
- black fine-tip marker
- blue and red markers
- ruler

STEP ONE

Cut the toilet-paper roll 3 inches tall, wrap with white paper, and glue it into place. Punch holes and push a skewer through, about ¾ inch from the top of the roll. This will keep the arms in place.

STEP TWO

Wrap a small foam ball with tinfoil to create R2-D2's head. Firmly press the ball into the roll.

STEP THREE

Use a pencil to draw the details of the body. Then trace it with a fine-tip black marker, filling in some areas with blue marker.

STEP FOUR

For the head, use a fine-tip marker to trace out the shapes on a separate piece of white paper. Fill in with blue and red markers, cut them out, and glue them on.

STEP FIVE

Fold a piece of white paper in half, and glue together so it's extra strong. Draw the arms, making them the same height as the toilet-paper roll. Cut out the arms, and add details. Punch holes at the top, and feed them onto the skewer. Glue the ends of the skewer to keep the arms from falling off. May the force (and the power to flush) be with you!

#98 MINECRAFT CREEPER

CRAFTS

Supplies needed

- 3 toilet-paper rolls
- scissors
- craft glue
- green paint
- paintbrush
- black, light, medium, and dark green construction paper

STEP ONE

Create a 3-D rectangle by folding one toilet-paper roll in half twice. Then cut two cubes (one slightly smaller than the other), and insert the smaller cube inside the larger cube to create the head.

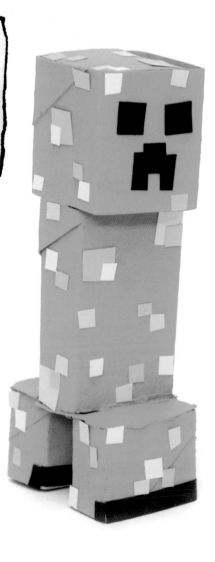

STEP TWO

Create another 3-D rectangle with the second roll. Turn it into a hexagon by flattening two of the opposite sides. Cut one of the shorter corners, and glue the flap underneath, creating a flat 3-D rectangle (it should be half as thick as the head). Cut the body to be a little longer than the head.

STEP THREE

From the third roll, cut a piece the width of the body. Cut open the piece, and press it flat to create a platform. Cut a rectangle three times the depth of the body. Make a thin 3-D rectangle (like the body in step 2). Finally, cut the thin rectangle into two smaller rectangles (about $2/3$ the height of the head). These are the legs.

STEP FOUR

Glue the head, body, and legs together as shown. Paint two coats of green paint over the entire Creeper, letting each coat dry for 10 minutes.

STEP FIVE

To make the pixels, cut tiny green squares of paper in various shades. To make the feet, cut two thin rectangles and four small squares of black paper. For the face, cut black squares for the eyes, nose, and mouth, and glue them on. Attach the long rectangles to the front of both legs. Then glue the squares to the sides of both legs. Finally, pixelate the Creeper by gluing the green squares on the body. Next time you need to stare down a green poo, you know who to call!

#99 CASTLE

CRAFTS

Supplies needed

- cardboard box
- scissors
- paint
- paintbrush
- 10 toilet-paper rolls
- washi tape
- black and brown markers
- toothpick

STEP ONE

Find a thin cardboard box, such as an empty cracker or cookie box. Lay it on its side, and cut off the front. Paint the box, and let it dry for 30 minutes.

STEP TWO

Cut tabs at the top at the top of each roll of toilet paper. Make some of the towers round and some square. Once the tabs are cut, paint the towers. Cut slits on both sides of each roll.

STEP THREE

Slide the towers onto the edges of the cardboard box. At the top of each tower, add some washi tape. (If you don't have washi tape, use paint.) Use a marker to add bricks on each tower.

STEP FOUR

Finish the castle by drawing a door with a brown marker. Use more washi tape and a toothpick for your castle's flag. Welcome to Poo Palace!

#100 MARBLE RUN WATERSLIDE

Supplies needed

- 11 toilet-paper rolls
- scissors
- white, blue, and green paint
- paintbrush
- hot glue
- craft knife
- flat cardboard box (such as a pizza box)

STEP ONE

Cut a slit on both sides of each toilet-paper roll, and then connect them. You can make them as tall as you want. This castle uses three toilet-paper rolls for the tallest tower, two for the second, and one and a half for the shortest tower.

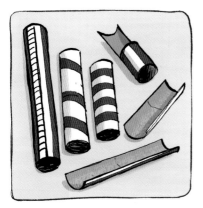

STEP TWO

Paint each tower white. Once the paint is dry, add some designs. Then, cut three toilet-paper rolls in half, and glue the ends together to create the slides. For the last slide, make a tunnel by only cutting away the top part of the toilet-paper roll. Paint the outside of the slides white and the insides blue. Let the paint dry.

STEP THREE

Ask an adult for help to cut holds in the towers for the slides, using a craft knife. Glue the slides in place. Make sure to tilt the slides down so the marbles will roll easily.

STEP FOUR

A cardboard pizza box works well as a base for the marble run. Paint the base with green paint, and let it dry. Glue the towers to the cardboard box.

STEP FIVE

Cut a small square at the end of your slide for the marbles to drop into. Then make a door on the side of the box, so the marbles can easily roll out. Add a little pool at the base of the slide with blue paint. Remember—no peeing in the pool!

#101 SURPRISE CRACKER

CRAFTS

Supplies needed

- wrapped treats
- scissors
- toilet-paper roll
- tissue paper
- craft glue
- ribbon
- scrapbook paper

STEP ONE

Fill the toilet-paper roll with your favorite wrapped treats! Cut a piece of tissue paper a little longer than the roll and glue it in place.

STEP TWO

Cut two pieces of ribbon, and tie each end of the tissue paper. Cut a piece of scrapbook paper, a little shorter in length than the roll, and glue it over the tissue paper. Surprise! You've done 101 things while you pooed!